# The Way to God

SHER GILL Galib

Grosvenor House
Publishing Limited

This book is published by
Grosvenor House Publishing Ltd
Link House
140 The Broadway, Tolworth, Surrey, KT6 7HT.
www.grosvenorhousepublishing.co.uk

A CIP record for this book
is available from the British Library

Paperback ISBN 978-1-80381-168-0
Hardback ISBN 978-1-80381-169-7
eBook ISBN 978-1-80381-170-3

This book first published: 10-2-2011

Website: www.shergill.uk.com
Email: beingasaint@gmail.com

SHER GILL Galib

# CONTENTS

Introduction                                    ix

In The Beginning                                 1
Seeker                                           8
Masters                                         11
Individual Path                                 21
Meditation                                      24
Deep Samadhi                                    27
Divine Light & Sound                            29
Karma                                           35
Five Passions of the Mind                       43
Dreams                                          49
Heart-Chakra                                    58
Dream Symbols                                   60
Fasting                                         63
Feeling                                         67
Patience                                        69
Purity                                          72
Harmony                                         75
The Temple or Fire Within?                      77
Illusion / Maya                                 80
What is Telepathy?                              85
Initiations / Dikhsha                           87

| | |
|---|---|
| Living in the Present Moment | 90 |
| Love | 95 |
| Miracles | 98 |
| Mind | 102 |
| Possession | 109 |
| Jealousy | 111 |
| Dark Night of the Soul | 114 |
| Depression | 117 |
| Curse | 122 |
| Heaven or Hell? | 124 |
| Power | 128 |
| Prince or Pauper | 133 |
| Let It Go | 137 |
| Destiny | 138 |
| Astrology | 143 |
| Love all Life | 149 |
| Abortion | 155 |
| Marriage | 160 |
| Will I Ever Be Happy? | 165 |
| Security | 169 |
| Problems Are Zero | 172 |
| The Real Age of Humans | 174 |
| Terrorism | 178 |
| Soul Mate | 182 |
| Who Is Vegetarian? | 185 |
| Saints | 188 |
| Oracles | 194 |
| Spiritual Scriptures | 197 |
| Religious Beliefs | 204 |

Soul Travel                                209

The Master Technique                       214

Self-Realisation                           223

Satnam Ji                                  228

Spiritual Wisdom                           236

Spiritual Healing                          240

To God: No competition                     244

Celebrities                                246

The Sadness of the Master                  248

Internet                                   250

Health                                     255

Death                                      262

The Riddle of God                          266

The Will of God                            270

Baba Nand Singh Ji                         273

God-Realisation                            276

Who Am I?                                  282

Anami-Lok                                  285

Spiritual Master and I                     287

Experience                                 291

The Seeker Is a Failure                    295

The Power of assumption                    298

# INTRODUCTION

This book results from pure dedication and struggles to find God. The spiritual writings of past saints inspired me to follow in their footsteps. I believed in them and felt it was possible to experience God in this lifetime. My inner search began at a very early age. This burning desire made me carry on seeking until I was satisfied. I was a severe religious follower and met with many storytellers. Talking alone about food does not satisfy hunger.

I approached and met many saints. I soon learned they were merely preachers who had mastered the writings of their respective religions and were fluent in the verses. When you ask any question, they often give evasive answers. A serious student of any religion has many questions to which they seek answers. With this in mind, I have tried to answer as many questions as possible in this book.

You will hardly find these answers anywhere. I have used layman's language to make my answers as simple as possible. I am sure you will find the answers you have been seeking. If the information you are seeking is not in this book, I urge you to read it with an open mind and contemplate your questions. I assure you that; Spirit will give the answers directly.

No one has the authority to change the names of the Gods' world or respective lords and rulers. During my travels, I have met with these beings; I have used their original names that may seem familiar to other religious writings. It does not mean I am offering a copy of them. My name is Sher Gill. It will remain the same in this world and higher worlds. Any spiritual traveller who has access to these higher worlds has the right to visit these regions and meet with their respective rulers to further their spiritual studies.

The information gained will not be the same; it may seem familiar. That, I believe, is purely coincidental. I have been trying to write this book for the last twenty-eight years but I have never managed it up until now. As they say, 'Tomorrow never comes.' Recently, I realised that if I did not write now, I would be wasting valuable knowledge. I am sure many people will read and benefit from it.

We all believe that God is within and has its presence within each soul. We create distance when we search for this presence, as it is a million miles away. When someone has any success, we arrogantly refuse to believe them. It shows how contradictory we are in our religious beliefs. We are the creation of God. It is the reason it lives and breathes through each of us. It has created a veil over our senses, so we cannot see or feel it directly. There are ways and means of clearing this mist.

The lower worlds are the school for the soul. Each soul is a replica of God yet individual in its way. God wants it to come back as an assistant in the higher worlds upon maturity of the soul. We all have families and hold religious congregations. That is fine in this world but the higher world approach is an individual act. The soul is alone but not lonely, so the path to God is unique.

The struggle becomes much easier with the help of a spiritual Master. The trial-and-error methods are laborious and success may never come. If you are sincere and have the desire to feel the presence of God, it makes no difference where you live in this world; between God and soul, there is no distance. It just is, within yourself and yet everywhere.

I wish you all success.

# IN THE BEGINNING

**God**

I am,

I am the one

I was the one.

I will be the one; Omnipotent (powerful), omniscience (knowing) and omnipresence (present). Every being in the universe is me and all beings are also thee. I am the beginning and end. The continuity of isness everlasting till me.

I am the creator and the creation is me. The cycle includes atmospheres, solar systems and universes, link by link in a chain. The Sun and moon worlds, down to earth, top to bottom; you are the centre of it and the centre is me. There was no rush to create this creation; I am beyond time. The heavens were manifested, beginning from me to you and from you to me.

All levels of beingness; Anami, Agam, Hakikat, Alaya, Alakh, Soul Plane and to the lower worlds. The time track, boundaries to cross and the chains are applied. Excitements to cries in the etheric to the mental, causal, astral and physical plane. The total consciousness is in iota to the mountains. The Spirit is everywhere; all in all is Spirit. The atmosphere of every corner, in and out and within, the Spirit breathes in and the Spirit breathes out.

It is inflow and outflow. It is divine light and sound. You can see me as light and can hear me as sound. Divine light and sound merge and become Spirit. That is the vehicle and you are the traveller to beingness and from beingness to me and I am always to you. There is no riddle. You make the riddle; you solve the riddle. The creation of souls came by reacting upon itself. So, the souls are part of God and I am the soul.

I am the experiencer and the experience is me. As the souls came from the creator to beingness, inexperienced in the lower worlds, they started from soil to minerals, birds to animals to humans. The journey has begun. Karmas are given as bank accounts to begin the activation. This activation led to multiplication and the game began. Nothing is difficult to understand. The key is beingness.

The rotation is twisting and it is turning fast. Undo one twist and it twists again, in the opposite direction, three times. The twist is on full speed and nonstop. Stop twisting or untwisting; let it be. Be still; no action, no thought, everything unfolds like a flower. The flower opens and blooms its fragrance into the atmosphere. The people have heard the message and come in flocks to hear. The school is open.

The Master appears to those who are ready and are the chosen ones. He can come in many ways; word of mouth, books, live appearances or a simple nudge. A whisper in the ear and the presence is strong. The vibrations are so fine and the fragrance is beyond description. You know it is here. You feel like you are about to fly; your feet are on the ground but your head is in the sky. You are in this world but not of it.

You are about to say I am; I am, I am it and it is me. The journey has begun. The Trinity is; God as Spirit and represents itself as the Master. There is always one Master of 'The Way to God' who represents God and there are many more Masters who also help. The Master is the way; without the Master, there is no path and nowhere to go. Souls will wander, without direction, with no mission in life, going around in circles with no end in sight.

It will be the endless wheel of eighty-four. The key is the Master. You can pop out of the unbreakable circle. When you do, you will realise and ask yourself; 'Where am I? You will know you have been here all the time. You are out and you are within. There is nowhere to go. Wherever you are, you are always the centre of it. You are the assistant and you are the Master. You are the prince and you are the heir to the throne. You are the experience and the experiencer.

God is God, it is the totality, it is the immense void that has no end, it is a big circle, it has shape and it has no form. The whole, the totality, is God itself. It is the big circle alone and it has millions, billions, trillions, atoms, particles and souls. All the atoms were not doing much, lying about in the suspension, totally dependent on God, the superior one. God has begun a new and exciting game. There are ascending and descending planes in this circle, higher and lower planes.

The vibrations run from fine to coarse. Souls are coming from Anami-lok to the soul plane to earth. All souls are within the circle; without this circle, there is no survival. This time, they are in the circle but they can roam as freely as they wish to create karma. They can go round and round on the wheel of eighty-four and are given independence to be

3

their boss. They struggle as they wish. The knower becomes the unknown. The curtain is drawn; the circus has begun.

In the beginning, it was the Golden-Age. Creativity and action were slow. Kal power was not fully awake. The souls were not creating much bad karma. Natural food for physical survival was provided. Even today, it is available. People have become ignorant and dependent on artificial food. This is the reason for excessive sickness. There were natural foods to eat. Caves and trees were provided for survival but there was little to do.

The pace of life was slow. Spiritual progress was slow. What we can achieve today in a few days, months or years took centuries in the olden days. The lifespan was long too; a few centuries to a few thousand years. I recall three thousand years in one body. Saints lived extra-long lives. People believed in meditation. They were guided to meditate. People believed in leading a saintly life. The spiritual eye was pretty active. Inner communication was strong.

We were in tune with nature and nature was in tune with us. The action and reaction were slow. There weren't many tests we could go through, unlike today. Soul was the chief and the five passions' activity was dull, almost unknown and spiritual progress was slow. There weren't many souls going back to the original creator. During the Silver-Age, the rate of vibrations as a whole changed.

The vibrations are now slightly more to the negative side. The soul receded somewhat into the background and the mind and physical body became more active. The spiritual eye also began to fade away. We had three eyes. Two were physical, as they are today, used to communicate with the

4

physical; one was spiritual, used to communicate within spiritual worlds. The third-eye was a natural gift bestowed upon us to communicate with our creator.

God said; you are far away on the physical but you can call me anytime and I am here. We are two and we are one. I am out and I am within. I am macrocosm and microcosm. Wherever you are, I am here.' Seeking God was not on the agenda except for a few because the atmosphere was almost godlike. People did not feel much urge to leave the physical. In that era, very few souls progressed spiritually and went back to the Godhead to become assistants to God.

The more experienced a soul is when going back to the creator, the more powerful it becomes. The more educated and civilised we are, the better the society is. Lower worlds are replicas of the higher worlds. The difference is the rate of vibration. The saints are believed to have higher, purer vibrations. These are the type of souls needed to become assistants with God.

Knowing that everyone is a saint, 'Can you imagine the society they have created? They are called higher worlds and these saints are the real assistants of God. The more intelligent or reliable the children, the more parents can relax. We should all strive to achieve this spiritual attainment. We have the qualities; we have the spark. We are part of it, the ocean of love and mercy.

We are supposed to breathe Spirit in and breathe Spirit out. With every step you take, with neutrality, you should feel that I am it and it is me. You are the Spirit; inner is the key. The repetition of the spiritual word is continuous, each day and night. Inner action is the key and the physical self is bound to follow. Wherever you are spiritually, that is where you are physically. Prepare yourself at the inner.

Watch every move and ask yourself if you are at it all the time. If you are, the mind and other bodies are just servants. They will follow commands naturally. The more active our minds and other bodies are, such as the causal, astral and physical, the more the inner self will fade into the background and it will not have much to express as a spiritual being. The person's actions will be emotional or physical and you will be further from your spiritual achievement.

The more spiritually active we are, the better people we are and better the assistants of God we are. It was the original purpose of sending souls into the lower worlds. As we unfold spiritually and return to the creator as active workers, we help God in its inner circle and feel better. As we are experiencing the help of God and it is experiencing itself through us at the same time.

It is the continued, everlasting circle of inflow and outflow. We travel outwardly and we travel inwardly; the vehicle is sound. The return of souls to the original home was on the move but it was slower than today. The creation is finished but the progression from the lower elemental to the higher being is moving. It is in the state of consciousness from the lower to the highest. We are all the same as souls but different in our consciousness.

We are all the same, from humans to animals, birds, insects and fruits, from a blade of grass to stones, tiny eggs, fishes and whales. They are all states of consciousness on different levels which is the difference between animals and humans. Humans have unfolded more spiritually than animals. Perhaps we have been here on this planet longer by the measure of time but eventually, they will catch up and progress to saintly positions one day. Then, they too will become assistants of God.

It is a very long process. That is why it is called the 'Wheel of Eighty-Four.' It is the approximate time for each soul to experience being an assistant in the presence of God. This cycle is of eighty-four hundred thousand lives. Some souls have progressed spiritually; they are gone but keep coming back again and again by their free will and the will of God. They are spiritual Masters.

They choose to help the Supreme Being and guide the souls back to God's world to be part of a spiritual society. The Master is the guru. The Master is a friend. The Master is the shower of the way. Without the Master, nothing is possible. Imagine a flock of sheep without a shepherd. We owe everything to the Master.

Without the Master, the paths are like dark alleyways.

# SEEKER

A Seeker is a person who has a spiritual yearning within. This yearning keeps the Seekers on their toes mentally as they search for something missing in their lives. It is called spiritual hunger. When the soul is ready, it begins its search for the creator. The mind and body follow the soul's inner dictates and the person becomes the Seeker. It does not matter if you are rich or poor; this internal yearning keeps you on the move.

Age is of no concern. It is the result of spiritual progress from our previous lives. On that basis, you could become a Seeker at a very early age, as soon as you come to your senses in this world. These people are blessed and they are here to fulfil God's mission. The search could be straightforward and sometimes it is very tiresome. If you are sent for a spiritual mission, then, in time, the Master will be there to receive you, take you under his wing and train you further.

If you are just approaching this milestone, your search will be according to your level of unfoldment. You could be satisfied with black magic or your level could be of psychic phenomena and finally, there is a search for the high, which is the temple within. The depth of yearning will express its needs. The Seeker is like the moth that is always searching for light. Upon finding the beloved light, it gives up its life for it.

When we meet our creator, we become more alive than ever before. First, we seek spiritual books. Most of the Seekers begin with the books and finish with the books. They cannot see any further than this, for they are not genuine Seekers. Once you are not satisfied with the book's knowledge, your next step will be to seek a living Master. Book knowledge is excellent but it cannot help you to cross the boundary line, whereas Master can.

The Master can explain things step by step and lead you to the inner when your approach has been external most of the time. Searching outside, we will only find its reflection, while the truth or reality lies within ourselves. The true Master will always lead you to the inner. There are many pseudo-masters. Very rarely will you catch a glimpse of a true Master, as they stay out of the limelight.

If you find a true Master, it is worthwhile as a Seeker. If not, move on until you meet the one you were searching for. When you see him, your inner will tell you, 'Yes, this is the one' and your journey begins. I was Seeker once and one of a kind. I was not easily satisfied, so my Master had to be one of a kind. I went through some studies at different levels and connected with other Masters.

When I met my spiritual Master, the search was over. I knew what I was searching for and I came to know what he could offer upon meeting him. Our friendship began as a Master and Seeker. You will be surprised to know your Master is also a Seeker but of another kind. He is searching for ready souls. When the soul is ready, the Master creates the situation whereby the soul will meet the Master in person.

Some Seekers are following the method of trial and error. The dangers of this method are numerous and the traps will be everywhere. The Seeker without a Master's protection can be taken as a wandering soul and trapped by hostile entities. If not guided by a Master, access to spiritual worlds will be very limited and his shield of protection will not be there.

Some experiences for the soul can be shocking and lead to mental disturbance. Suppose any success does happen and you have an out-of-body experience. In that case, the body is left behind, totally unprotected and wandering entities will be looking for this opportunity to occupy the body. When you come back to your body, which is also controlled by the occupying entity, the result can be disastrous; mental psychosis can result.

Play the safe game and never rush into anything.

# MASTERS

It is one of the essential subjects in the life of a spiritual Seeker. Without a living Master, nothing is possible. To be in the presence of the Master is one thing but to be known by the Master is another, especially at the spiritual level. Without these Masters, no religion in existence would have been possible. 'Could there have been Buddhism without Buddha, Islam without Mohammad, Christianity without Jesus, Sikhism without the ten Gurus and Hinduism without Krishna?

All living Masters were responsible for making these fantastic teachings available to us. The Masters mentioned above brought the teachings to us with fresh and improved ideas. It is why old religions are gone and forgotten. If people think no new religions are coming, all teachings are now out in the open and nothing more can be said about God; they are wrong. Most people cannot even grasp what already has been said or written about God and its creation.

There is nothing that people cannot understand. Most of the spiritual writings are not understood today. It is not the spiritual writings that you don't understand; the main barrier is the old language which does not exist. Once you understand this point, then there is no looking back. God is infinite and there is no end to its knowledge. The right person can bring new teachings to Earth.

All religious writings are not even one percent of the totality of the Supreme Being. The one who is omnipotent, omniscient and omnipresent. These are the three spiritual truths. There are Masters in this world who know so much but cannot express their knowledge openly because people are not ready to accept them. Most religions are against the living Master because they fear losing their followers. On the other hand, I don't blame them.

All living Masters are not true masters; many are pseudo-masters who have nothing to give to their followers. They have created systems to collect donations. When disturbed by problems, people are desperate to look for some security and walk into their traps. Some grow long hair, while others dress in orange and display certain symbols on their forehead. There is nothing wrong with this. They are attempting to look like holy men. They create this persona but it does not mean they are saints.

They have studied some religious books thoroughly and can express themselves well. Still, this does not put them in the same category as saints. They are only preachers. Most of the people I come across tell minor stories which happened ten thousand years ago. Most of these stories are nothing but myths. Most people listen to and enjoy what they say because they cannot see any other avenue.

It shows that people are not ready to step forward and accept new changes. One day, change will come and most religions will go into the shadow, especially those struggling today. When a person seeks to follow any Master, they should seek sufficient information about him. 'What does he teach and what have you heard about him? 'Do you know someone who can verify who he is? 'Finally, does his teachings suit and satisfy your spiritual need?

If the answer is 'yes,' go ahead and follow him; otherwise, move on and seek further until you find someone who has the answers to all your questions. 'You also have a duty as a Seeker to ask yourself if your needs are spiritual or materialistic? If your needs are materialistic, then you are wasting the time of a good Master. The true Master is the representative of God in this world.

God cannot talk or walk into someone's house to express its presence. However, it expresses itself in every single atom in the entire universe. People are not ready and most of them are ignorant in believing any of this. They think everything is for their use and nothing is behind the running of this universe. God must show its presence on earth, not directly but indirectly, so it chooses a messenger in a physical embodiment.

He is not an ordinary person but has been trained for many incarnations and built up to a certain spiritual level. He can receive God's spiritual message and express it verbally or through his writings to the Seekers. He is the light of this world. He is the light giver. He looks, talk, walk and lives just like anyone else. His state of consciousness makes him stand out from the rest. Most of his work is done silently. He is a guardian of the truth.

No one can understand what he does unless he wants them to know with his own free will. He can live a life without any trace of himself. He teaches only to a few in his circle and protects the world as a whole. Teaching people in the open is one of his duties but there are more significant duties to perform in the inner world. The true Master always teaches divine light and sound. Without these, his followers will be at a spiritual standstill.

It will bring inner discipline, which is more important than physical discipline. If the inner is ready, then the outer will follow automatically. This is how it works. This is the setback with most religions today; They prepare themselves on the outer as much as possible and do nothing about the inner. They do not progress spiritually; this is their failure point. It does not matter how much knowledge you have physically.

Without light and sound, nothing is possible. Light and sound are our inner communication. There is always a plus point and everything is beyond limits. We also call the Master a spiritual traveller. He links us with light and sound to have success in spiritual travelling. Divine light and sound are our primary instruments to communicate with God but without the Master's guidance, we never become aware of them. He builds up the spiritual foundation on which we become successful.

His other means to represent the teachings are written discourses and books. The Seeker must put enough effort, so the Master's effort is not wasted. It is teamwork. The spiritual shield of the Master is provided to all Seekers for protection. It prevents any attack by entities always looking for psychically open people. He travels with you in the inner worlds and protects your physical body as it becomes an empty shell.

The Master makes sure no harm can come to your physical body. The Master in the physical is limited but he can create two or three other physical bodies if necessary. However, as a spiritual Master, he can create millions of spiritual bodies and be with all his Seekers across the world. He is the true representative of God on earth and God gave him the power to be everywhere at any time. I witnessed this, as I had seen my Master many times in England when physically he was in America.

This is the role of the Master to teach while the Seeker's part is to learn. It is satisfying when the Master teaches and the Seeker learns. Spirituality cannot be taught but can be caught. Spiritual wisdom comes from the Master like a cat on silent feet. 'Can you hunt it? You must learn to hunt before you can claim to be a hunter. Before you become a hunter, you have to be hunted by the Spirit first. This is all possible with the help of the Master.

What I have mentioned so far is nothing. There are people who always protest against these God-sent men because they haven't got a clue about these Masters and their mission in this world. They are telling others to do the same. They are misled and are misleading others. This is their strong point, controlling the masses. Despite all their efforts, genuine Seekers will find their way to the truth. The Masters found success because they left religious systems to discover the truth.

All world religious temples are run by the systems. I have never seen anyone spiritually successful who followed these systems. Suppose you do find success that will be limited as well. As long as you are part of any system, you will be for or against other religious bodies. Guru Nanak, Buddha and many others left the old systems and found success. In return, we appreciate what they have left for us. I have learned a lot from my Master's. Everything I know today was gifted by him.

You can see the success in his teachings and can say with awe, 'What a teacher!' Without my Master's, I don't think I would have known as much. My writing is limited; I know more but cannot express it in writing, knowing no religious man will accept it. The Master can take you from the physical to the highest plane, known as Anami-Lok. Guru Nanak was one of the best spiritual travellers of the fifteenth century.

Being the representative of God, the Master loves all life very dearly but if someone tries to damage something in this world, he will not stop them or change their mind. He lets them commit negative karma because changing someone's mind is against the spiritual law. He does nudge you, as a feeling, letting you know that you will do wrong. If the follower ignores it and goes ahead and makes a mistake, then the Seeker is responsible for its actions.

The Seeker should be ready to pay back as soon as possible. Most of us do want to learn the hard way. The Master helps all Souls who cry out during big disasters, such as earthquakes. He even tries to prevent them if possible. In Asia, the tsunami of 26 December 2004 destroyed many islands and 229,000 people lost their lives. Usually, a disaster such as an earthquake occurs at ground level; however, this time it came out of the sea. It was a build-up of bad karma as a whole on these islands.

I do not have to mention what kind of bad karma they committed. Most civilised people will know what was going on, on these islands. When the build-up of karma goes past its limit, these disasters are inevitable and many innocent people and children will suffer. The Masters are oceans of kindness. It is one of their virtues. They are here to give the blessings of God on its behalf.

The Masters are the greatest healers on this Earth. I have at least one hundred different cases in my personal file where I requested healing and received it within twenty-four hours.

I asked for healing on behalf of other people, with their permission and they too were instantly healed. Many people came from different religions to ask if I could request healing on their behalf without fail and the healings were given.

People try their religions first and when nothing happens, they cry out for help. Not in a single instance did I send written requests., I thought of the problem and the people involved; they received healing. In the worst-case scenarios, I went into meditation and did the job. I did nothing and I have never given credit to myself. It was the Master who did it. All I can say is that he has never let me down. That is the true Master.

The Master stands alone in this world. He does not break any laws and does not recommend his followers do so. He disagrees with many laws but they are physical laws made to control uncivilised people. The Master is beyond all these laws; he is a law unto himself. He has his way of doing things. He is in complete authority in this universe and beyond but he does not interfere if possible.

The Master never harms anyone, not even a tiny fly, as he is the protector. The people who try to harm the Master should be prepared to reap what they sow. 'The mill of God grinds slowly but it grinds exceedingly well.' In the past, people have created heavy karma against the Master. I think now is the time to pay the Master back. The Master leaves everything to God and never asks for any concessions. As Jesus said, 'Father, forgive them, for they know not what they do.'

The Master always lives in God's will and requests the good of the whole. Masters cannot afford to harm anyone it is not in their nature. Masters do not perform any miracles purposely. It is left to the magicians who want to impress people. The land where the Master stands is blessed. Wherever they go, many changes take place due to the higher vibration they carry. Their aura is so positive that changes begin to materialise as they move about.

Miracles start to happen and people who come into the Master's aura are healed. Masters do not do it purposely; it just happens. The blind received sight, people suffering from pain are in pain no more, the list is countless. The Master's gaze upon the individual is more than enough and anything that comes to your mind at that particular time is done. I have seen this happen many times. No one can imagine the pure spiritual current Masters carry.

The Master teaches all his followers to detach from material things and the people who hold them back spiritually. Those who have given up in life can gain a sound knowledge of the soul itself. To discover your true identity as a soul is Self-realisation and knowing how God operates is God-realisation. The Masters are on different levels, according to their unfoldment. Some Masters operate up to the astral plane or soul plane and some have access to dwelling in the Ocean of Love and Mercy.

God chooses one Master as its embodiment to show its presence everywhere. The true Masters, especially those we discuss here, are rarely qualified according to the world's academic standards. These qualifications are not necessary. He does not want to be loaded with too much world knowledge. Most famous spiritual travellers we know hardly went to school. The scholars cannot understand the spiritual revelations they left behind because they had access to knowledge beyond the material world.

This is not in the grasp of today's education. All holy books at present do not comprise even one percent of the totality. What we know and express here are merely reflections of what lies beyond and even this reflection is represented in a diluted form. The Masters are and have been working very hard to bring this knowledge to the lower worlds so we can become Seekers and perhaps become future Masters too.

The Masters can have longevity if they have a special mission to fulfil. There is a secret behind their longevity; They use Spirit as food, more or less, to keep them healthy. As long as all the body atoms are healthy, the body does not grow old. Not everyone can access this spiritual food. I know someone who has kept his physical body for more than 561 years. I have been fortunate enough to meet him several times.

After serving God according to their allotted time, they make sure they have trained someone in the world who can take their place. The new person could be anywhere in the world. This true teaching does not and will not stay in one country or people working in the same office previously supervised by the descended Master. We cannot limit these teachings. This is why the new Master can be from any part of the world. This is for the good of the whole.

The present Master hands over spiritual power to the new Master in the presence of Spirit; the time and dates are chosen accordingly. We cannot set a particular time or date, as the passing over of Spirit is beyond limits. Spirit will take its course and God decides to keep the teachings open or keep them a secret.

'One' God-sent Master is always present in this world. There is no such time when he has not been around. Before leaving this physical world, my Master passed on the spiritual responsibility so that I might carry on. Some have accepted me as a spiritual Master, while many have remained undecided. It is not important to be known by millions.

This is the way Masters work

# INDIVIDUAL PATH

On this path, spiritual teachings are according to your state of consciousness. The individual means the immortal self, the spark of God. The Way to God; teachings are not for the masses or preachers who go door to door to convince people to follow us. This way, we invade someone's psychic space and tell them we are better than you are. Anyone who follows this principle violates spiritual law and clearly states that our teachings are for the masses.

All mass teachings are based on the welfare of this world. To improve the physical side of the individual or bring peace and heaven on earth will never happen. It is a reasonably exciting dream to have. Peace on earth is essential and I wish it would stay on the ground forever. I admire the people working towards this cause but as long as people are greedy and hungry for power, they will never let this happen.

We should be interested in the soul's welfare, which is individual in its way. God has created it individually and it retains its individuality throughout eternity. It does not matter which plane it is on or which physical embodiment it is using. The soul is permanent, while the physical body is temporary and dies after every lifespan. To gain more experience, the soul goes through the reincarnation system and at birth, it takes a new physical body as a child.

We learn as the child grows into old age and dies but the soul gains the experience and lives forever. If we know the physical body is temporary, 'Why do we care about its welfare? We need to take care of the soul, which is permanent and is the experiencer with unfoldment. The soul unfolds spiritually and becomes aware of its presence during each incarnation. When before, our mind was the Master.

Now the soul is aware and the mind also matures spiritually and it feels the internal nudge that indicates; I am not part of the masses. It feels and says, 'Therefore that I am.' That is the first step to realise its individuality. Now it seeks spiritual freedom from the incarnation system. No two souls are at the same spiritual awareness. We all vary from one another. The difference is in the experience gained over several lifespans.

If our state of consciousness is different, then our spiritual teachings will be individual. We cannot sit in the same class and make further progress. We can sit in the same Satsang, which is held once every month but we need a teacher capable of teaching each individual according to their level. This spiritual experience gained over many lives is your personal and it cannot be divided or shared by other family members as we share other material things.

No one can take away the experience, which is stored in your soul records. This maturity makes us the Seeker and you know for sure that you are no longer part of the crowd. The Master looks at your soul records and begins to educate you from that point onwards. Every soul is dealt with individually and education is based on their capabilities. We are individuals on many bases; we were born alone, experience and die alone.

Very rarely are two individuals the same in this world. Our unfoldment makes us different from each other and we seek according to that. It is the struggle of the soul into the lower worlds to find its true identity. If you have not come to the point where you realise that you are not part of the crowd, then you have not gone too far up the spiritual ladder.

God is alone and has given you its qualities, which are also alone. You are an individual and yet part of it. This is what we will experience to become active assistants of God. Whereas, before we struggled to find our true identity as souls, we are now part of God and an individual.

You are the experience and the experiencer.

# MEDITATION

What you want to follow in life is an individual choice. God has invested spiritual power in the soul and you can activate it at the pineal gland, also known as the third-eye. All psychic powers sit silently in our lower chakras. 'Are you interested in psychic powers or pure spiritual experience? The lower powers can be materialised through different means; magic spells or controls. Each chakra has its powers.

It is a laborious and slow process. The practitioner can spend a long time on one chakra alone and it may take a lifetime to go through half the chakras successfully unless your guru is good and the Seeker is ready. If the Seeker is ready, then it is possible to achieve this in a short period. Still, we are talking about a few years before the successful candidate can make it to the Crown-Chakra.

The final journey for the meditation practitioner is the Crown-Chakra. 'Will it work out successfully? There is no guarantee. It applies to the people who begin their practice from lower chakras. Those who practice under the supervision of a guru may begin their practice at the third-eye and find success through the Crown-Chakra. Those who practice at lower chakras without any Master could get in trouble. The lower chakras can wake up and originate psychic powers, bringing fatal results.

The person could be mentally disturbed and psychically controlled by the entities involved. The powers are great but if psychic phenomena are created for material gain or to impress others, it will be very difficult to get out of that habit. It is like show business; Once you experience the limelight, you cannot do without it. It is a good achievement but you have to decide your goal in life.

Do you want to achieve psychic powers and remain in the creativity of the lower worlds or 'Are you interested in God's world and going beyond the dividing barrier into the pure spiritual worlds? People who approach psychic worlds only and consider this the end of everything have not even scratched the surface of spirituality. In the beginning, every practitioner has to go through lower worlds.

It would help clear your karmas on each plane to reach up to the soul plane and above. The Master instructs the Seeker not to get involved in the lower chakras or lower worlds. For this reason, the phenomena are seen and the capability to create phenomena is limited. Even if psychic powers come as you travel through the lower worlds, the Master controls them. We, the inexperienced, can get excited about these phenomena, which is another pitfall on the way to God.

Some Seekers get discouraged because they do not see or cannot seem to do anything as exciting as this. They may label this path as boring and it is not true. Some of them drift back to their old beliefs. This way, their spiritual journey is halted and they have to wait for a similar opportunity in future life. In the beginning, you may put attention on the pituitary gland, between the eyebrows base of the nose and leads up to the pineal gland.

See the chapter on **soul travel** for its correct position. The pituitary gland is the seat of the mind, while the pineal gland is the seat of the soul. That is the difference between these two glands. When we focus on the pituitary gland, the process of attention is through the **imagination**, which is a tool of the mind. Our mind is the instrument of mental faculties.

Then we come to the pineal gland area, which is the seat of the soul. As we know, the soul is a unit of God-awareness. Once it becomes aware of itself, it can shift itself through the narrow passage leading to the Crown-Chakra. This is on top of the head, also known as the soft spot. It is visible on children's heads or the spiritual people who purposely keep it open to have frequent journeys into the spiritual worlds.

The soul can also use other spiritual openings to leave the body. Once you have attained success with practice, you will know what works best for you. Other bodies become active during your spiritual travels and the silver cord limits you. Each body has its limits for visiting different planes. Also, in early travels, you will experience stomach pain if you venture too far but soon, you will get used to it.

It is recommended to travel internally or externally via the soul, which is beyond the limits of the silver cord. The silver cord limits you only up to the etheric plane; beyond this, the soul is free. External travel is a phenomenon to satisfy your mind and impress others. Inner travel or the state of being is the actual achievement and the way forward to the spiritual worlds.

The choice is yours

# DEEP SAMADHI

'What is deep samadhi? This is a widespread question that arises among new Seekers and others who have not been through this experience yet. This is a unique experience and will clear many doubts from the Seekers who believe that they have fallen asleep during their meditation period. In the early days, I had my doubts and thought I was wasting my time during each session.

During meditation, I used to fall asleep the same as everyone else. I went to see someone who was more senior than I was in the spiritual field. The answers I received from this person were not very satisfactory, so I came home a bit disappointed. Somehow, I knew there was more to it than sleep within myself. My meditation time was approaching in the evening, so I thought, 'Why not ask the Master? At the beginning of my meditation, I requested the spiritual Master to clear this point.

I began my meditation as usual. After a short while, I fell asleep again but the Master woke me up to show me what was taking place during this period known as sleep. He made me conscious enough physically to understand what was happening while I was still in the middle of the experience.

What I witnessed was incredible. My mouth was completely shut; the word I was chanting at the beginning of the exercise and now it was rolling within. It was on a continuous roll, with such a rhythm, without fail. I wished to keep on listening but Master retook me into meditation when he knew I was satisfied. Your word begins to chant itself without making any physical or mental effort. This is called true meditation, also known as deep samadhi.

This is what happens when doing spiritual exercises with full sincerity. It is an effortless effort and all your mental activities vanish. With the blessings of the Master, everything is possible. Without the Master, 'Who would you request or wake you up during the middle of the meditation to show you what was taking place?

There are three stages of meditation.

**First:** In the beginning, you are trying to chant a spiritual word. You are conscious of this repetition and also of the surrounding noises. A few thought forms are still wandering around.

**Second:** You go into a rhythm. Your thoughts and surrounding noises vanish.

**Third:** You become unaware of yourself in the physical. This rhythm stops vocally and the word repeats itself within, on a continuous roll, until you become conscious of yourself again or the Master gives you a nudge, meaning time is up.

This is deep samadhi.

# DIVINE LIGHT AND SOUND

Divine light and sound are spiritual food for the soul. This is a means of survival for the soul. Without this food, the soul would wither away, just as the body weakens without food and dies from starvation. It is impossible with the soul, as the soul never dies, so God has created a way for its survival. The soul is constantly communicating with God but we are not aware of this communication because our mind is very active when the soul is silent.

Once our mind is under control and operates on a balanced state, the soul expresses its presence and we become aware of this communication. 'What is this communication? It is referred to as the Word by Christians, Anhad-Jap by Sikhism and various other names by most world-famous religions. Without light and sound, nothing could exist. Light and sound are the two pillars of God for expression and when light and sound merge, they become Spirit.

So, there is God as the father and Master as the son and essence as the Spirit. This is the trinity on which most of the true teachings are based. If one out of three is missing, it is called spiritually inactive religion. God has many ways of expressing itself. One of them is Spirit. It is through Spirit that God's presence is known and felt everywhere. Through Spirit, God communicates with the whole of its creation, right from the lower scale to the highest.

First, it is Spirit and then it splits into two and becomes light and sound. Now, through these two main attributes of God, the whole of creation is manifested. Everything we see is light and everything we hear is sound. Now, this is the reality. Light is also knowledge. 'What do we see first? We see each other. We see the sun, moon, stars, buildings, trees or any object we can think of or whatever is within our grasp.

It is all light. In reality, light is a spectrum with many different colours in its pure form. 'Why do things look different from each other? All materials look different because they are arranged differently from each other light-wise and all carry different vibration rates. All these materials are created by light and bonded by sound to be sustained together. The arrangement appears as materials according to our requirement when seen by the physical eyes.

According to their arrangement, when seen by or through the spiritual eye, they appear as different shades of light. In other words, everything is manifested with the help of light and sound, which provide the image; otherwise, everything will remain invisible. Now, this is the creation and expression of God on the visible side.

This kind of spiritual experience looks very simple when seen through the spiritual eye and shown by God's grace but expressing it on the physical plane is impossible. We can go around the subject but our expression will still be far away. This is even more difficult for the person who wants to understand what I am trying to express. I have seen it but the other person is trying to imagine what I have seen. So, it is complicated to draw a picture.

This is why, in the old days, saints used sign language, known as symbols. I don't think anyone can understand this kind of experience through symbols or written languages unless the experience takes place within. This is why the Master always says, 'Go within. There lie all the answers to your questions.'

Nowadays, we see all these colours expressed through shades of light, materials, etc. This is the effort of our scientists, who want to create something new. They ponder upon the idea day and night and for them, the experience opens up and they gather the idea and express it via the means available to them. So, the light is seen on the physical plane in numerous ways.

When the light is seen in the inner, it has its ways of expression, also numerous. We can see the light when doing our meditation. We can see the light in our dream state. It can also open up to us when we are in subconscious sleep or the awakened state. Few people can see the auras of other people. The light which appears around the person is always a different colour.

It depends on the state of consciousness of that person. If the person is feeling depressed, the colour of the light will be depressing, black or dark brown. For a spiritual person, it could be gold or pure white or maybe blue for intelligent or intellectual people. So, the light will express its colour according to the situation and state of consciousness.

As you go within and according to your journey, the light will present itself in different colours, according to the experience taking place; a pinkish colour on the astral plane, probably orange on the causal plane and blue on the mental plane. As said before, blue is of intellectuals and yellow or gold is of the soul plane. During your experience, if you do not remember anything but the colour, this will act as a yardstick to assure you mentally on which plane this experience has taken place.

The light is also spiritual knowledge when travelling within ourselves. We travel on sound and to see where we are going; we follow the light. It leads us from the physical to the soul plane and above. The light expresses our state of consciousness and acts like our passport. When seen by the lords of other planes and entry is granted. Light is the infinite expression of God and we are individual channels of it.

The soul journeys with light and sound into the lower worlds, also called the word. This is the way into the lower worlds and the way out of the lower worlds as soon as you find it. This world is like a maze; There is also a way out if there is a way in. Divine light and sound work together as a team. Light is knowledge, which we have earned with our effort and we become awakened souls.

This awakening leads us to hear the sound, which is constantly rolling within us, all the time, in different melodies. All these melodies are built within us by God. It is very similar to radio sound waves. As we tune into other channels, we can hear the sound. Each plane has its sound and we also have internal bodies according to each plane. The sound we hear indicates the awakening of internal bodies. For example, the sound of a flute suggests the awakening of the soul body.

The continuous rolling of these melodies is called sound, word or internal **dhun**. In Eastern teachings, it is recommended that you listen to this continuous **dhun** but unfortunately, not many people in this world can guide the follower to this experience. It is the same with followers; they want to listen to these melodies but have many indulgences in other avenues of life. They cannot listen, so it is more or less like the blind leading the blind.

The flow of sound is continuous from God through all planes to earth and returning to the Ocean of Love and Mercy. It is like two waves that are continuously moving. One is an outflow from the Ocean of Love and Mercy and the other is an inflow toward its creator. Soul travel is based on the inflow and outflow of waves. We travel on these inflow sound waves as we go within ourselves to have subjective experiences.

When we have accomplished the task, we return on the outflow sound waves back to our everyday human senses. This inflow or outflow can be in reverse order. It depends on whether we look from the physical side or God. It is more or less a continuous circle. While we have subjective experiences, we are mostly unaware of our physical surroundings or minor sounds unless somebody disturbs us or touches our bodies.

An evil disturbance could result in a startling awakening out of the experience and shock the experiencer. It can put the individual out of balance for days. So, it is always best to practice in a safe or isolated place, where disturbance is minimal. These sound waves, which we mentioned as inflow and outflow, are not just one or two. It is not like a bus stop, where you are waiting for the bus so you can jump in and take a ride.

These waves are continuously on the move and they are billions and trillions in number. They are manyfold greater in number than the total of God's creation. They are available for everyone to jump on all the time. This is why the spiritual melody is continuous within us.

We have some spiritual exercises if you prefer to follow the instructions and put enough time into practice. With practice, you can listen to this internal sound whenever you want. I have listened to this. When you are listening, you don't want to open your eyes. Sound is the greatest healer ever. The practitioner or the person who is an open channel for Spirit; by applying sound, can cure all the physical ailments of the sick person. Similarly, the application of light as well.

To see the sick person or to touch the person physically is not recommended or required but successful application of spiritual vibrations matters. The light and sound as Spirit is the food of the Eshwar-Khanewale (God-eaters). This is their food intake and the secret to their survival or longevity. So light and sound applied to the physical body for healing purposes bring vitality to the physical body.

It is written somewhere that sound is more important than light. It is not true. Both are equally important. To travel on the sound only is not possible. It is similar to walking with one's eyes closed. Sound is the vehicle or means of travel and light shows the spiritual path. Therefore, light and sound go hand in hand as a team or Spirit. All miracles we see are created through light and sound.

Light and Sound are the essences of God.

# KARMA

Karma is the central theory of life. The soul begins its journey from the soul plane to the lower worlds, it is given some karma by the Lord of Karma in the astral plane and its birth is arranged in the physical world. If karma is not provided for the soul, it will remain in the soul plane, karma-less and free. On the physical plane, it will go through eighty-four hundred thousand lives to gain experience to become karma-less once more to achieve spiritual freedom.

The creation is finished but the souls are created every day. These are two different theories. 'The creation finished' means that whatever God wanted to create in the lower worlds has already been created, such as; man, woman, animals, birds and insects. Now, whatever they may be, these creations are going through the multiplying process.

As you have noticed, the population of this world has increased enormously within the last hundred years. So, 'Where do these extra souls come from? During the times of Adam and Eve, there were only a few humans. They were not committing sins or not that many. The multiplying process was almost at a standstill. Then Adam and Eve sinned and the wheel of karma rolled.

This is similar to the automobile industry. It is a long process and involves the contribution of many people as a team to make a car. As they come down the production line, workers make hundreds and thousands of them, according to demand. Although all the cars look the same, each vehicle is given a unique chassis number to provide it with individuality.

Similarly, when souls are created, they all are individual. They all have their identities, known as spiritual names. On the same basis, their karma accounts are separate. The creator is everywhere but the process of creation is done on Anami-Lok. As new souls arrive on the soul plane, the spiritual process is followed so they can begin their experience on earth.

In the beginning, we create many karmas at a very high speed. When a child is born, it is helpless and incapable of earning its living. So, the parents accommodate and provide nutrition for the baby and whatever else it requires. So, at this stage, the child is on the receiving end.

The saints always guide us to give and not to receive. If we wish to improve our lives, leave this world forever and achieve spiritual freedom, we must unfold whatever we have done. We have to undo everything we have done over thousands of years. When people mention ten million or twenty million years, they make me laugh. They only say it because they feel better mentioning the word millions.

The process is long but not that long. If a blood sample is taken from any person who is fifty years old, scientists today are still unable to tell the exact age of that person. Leave the million-year theory to one side and only say how far you can go back and say it comfortably.

These are four main cycles of different times.

| | | |
|---|---|---|
| Satya-Yuga | (Golden-Age) | 1,728,000 years |
| Treta-Yuga | (Silver-Age) | 1,296,000 years |
| Dwapara-Yuga | (Bronze-Age) | 864,000 years |
| Kali-Yuga | (Iron-Age) | 432,000 years |

The total number of years is 4,320,000, known as Maha Yuga. These yugas are mentioned in the Hindu Vedas. At the end of Kali-Yuga, most souls will be able to make their way back home. The remaining ones will be taken back and live in a suspended or bliss state until a new earth planet is ready. The new yugas will begin again and these souls in a bliss state will be the new arrivals.

Suspension terminology is comparative to a bliss state, as souls do not sleep. Neither can they be destroyed. This world is still good enough for another four hundred thousand years. Many religions and pundits are forecasting the end of this world. These are the people who are creating cheap stunts or looking for publicity. Many dates have been given in my present lifespan, such as the millennium. 'But has this prediction or any other come true? The answer is **No,** so do not be bothered by these people in the future.

These are the ages of the four yugas mentioned by many religions. But some religions talk about this change of yugas whenever one of their respected saints or saviours were here. Unless they are talking about changing the yuga of Dwapara into Kali-Yuga. In that case, I entirely agree with what they say because Dwapara-Yuga changed into Kali-Yuga in 3,200 BC and you can add 2022 years, which brings us up to this year, for a total of 5,222 years.

Their spiritual writing is no older than ten thousand years with full respect to that religion. Therefore, all their religious or mythological stories should be based on Dwapara-Yuga and Kali-Yuga but they do mention Golden-Yuga as if it were here yesterday. Looking into the figures seriously, as mentioned in the previous paragraphs, we shouldn't have anything in written form in our possession, especially on the physical plane or the senses.

There is a place where all the records are kept from the beginning of time to the present. They are called the Nakal (copy) Records, the oldest records in existence. They are kept in one of the hidden spiritual cities on the physical plane. Any spiritual person can look or scan into these records at the Katsu-pari monastery.

Travelling can be done by soul internally or externally. This spiritual city is based in the Himalayan mountains. Fubi Kants is responsible for these records and the record-keepers are there too with a watchful eye. They also have special guards who guard this spiritual city. They are highly trained people and nobody can approach this spiritual city without their knowledge, as they can scan them to see their purpose of visit.

The entire process is spiritual, so the physical approach is totally out of the question. It is the atmosphere of that place and all psychic space is fully sealed. If someone is going that way, knowingly or unknowingly, they are diverted by creating illusory paths. Those people who are allowed inside are trustworthy and regular visitors. Some are known as spiritual teachers and they take their students there for study purposes.

Going back to Satya-Yuga, it was not as golden as mentioned in the spiritual scriptures. People were doing the wrong things, significantly less or not as often as we do today. If they were not doing anything wrong or creating karma, the process of karma would have stopped and we would not be in Kali-Yuga today. So, a small build-up on a gradual karma scale brought us to the present time. People were killing each other but not as often.

People would not cheat as often as today because most things, such as food and shelter, were provided for free by nature. Kal was working at a slow and steady pace in the atmosphere. The penetration of Kal power was tough to get through in people's minds, the presence of Kal was always there and it will always be here in the lower worlds because all these lower worlds are subject to the Kal power.

All the yugas are and were subject to the Kal power. During Satya-Yuga, the only difference is that people had better and easier access to spiritual information because third-eye was fully open. We could use the spiritual eyes and all the information was available. People preferred to have a natural approach to everyday life. The physical eyes were used as a regular part of daily living.

Souls were not going back to the soul plane because they had a lot to learn. For this purpose, spiritual Masters were sent into the lower planes. We know them as saints. Their purpose was to make people aware of spiritual activities and help them find their way back to the Godhead. What we can achieve today in a very short time took probably a few hundred years in Satya-Yuga.

In the Golden-Age, the lifespan was also a lot longer. As the yugas changed, the speed of karma became very fast. There are four main kinds of karma and each branch of karma has its extensions into millions. This is a vast subject and every soul in this universe is subject to one of the karmas below.

**Adi karma (prime karma):** These karmas were given to us by the Lord of Karma to begin our journey in the physical and activate the karma process.

**Aam karma (daily karma):** We create these karmas daily during our everyday life. It could be positive or negative karma; however, most of the time, it is negative karma. People love to be on the receiving end; therefore, our credit level goes down and we are in the area of debt. We weave our karma similar to Persian rugs, which are very hard to undo and we end up on the lower survival scale.

These daily karmas are worked off daily. If somehow, we are unable to work out these karmas in this life, then they will be carried with our soul records, mainly in the causal body and then they will become our fate karmas.

**Pre-Aam (fate karma):** This is something you have earned in one of your previous six lives but did not manage to pay back. These karmas are attached to us from birth.

Many people complain that they have never done anything wrong but they suffer. Your fate karma keeps creeping up since they need to be balanced and suddenly, the opportunity has come to pay it back. Do not feel discouraged. This is the law of karma or cause and effect.

'What is the cause? Somewhere in life, we start an action and it appears as a reaction at a later date. This is the law of the Lord of Karma, who keeps full records. You will be surprised to learn where he keeps all these records. This is why every individual soul is attached to the causal body. It acts as a storehouse of our past lives on the physical and astral plane. The subconscious body retains all the lower-plane records, where they can be scanned.

Today's computer systems are similar. We can store anything and by feeding in our passwords, we can unlock and transfer any information. Man has made the computer but the computer did not make the man. So, few awakened individuals worked their way into this field and found success. What we have seen so far is that there is a lot more yet to come. Everything we see or do is a replica of the astral plane. There is a museum where all past and future inventions are stored.

Spiritually awakened people go there in their dreams and their astral senses gain the information. The vibrations on the astral plane are more refined than on the physical. Those who can raise their vibrations will make their way in and have all the information they need. Do not be discouraged by fate karma. We are only paying back what we have borrowed.

**Sin-chet (reserve karma):** It is very similar to a savings account; the Lord of Karma can withdraw these karmas and dictate a person's life to say where they are to live. These people are not ordinary people. The Lord of Karma shifts these individuals for some purpose. Now we want to know, 'How do we create karma? There are five passions of the mind.

These five faculties are so strong that they will drag the individual to the lowest point possible and each faculty is also branched to another hundred, so it can work in a very subtle way. We need to learn how to balance these faculties to not drag us down to the animal level. That is also a negative thought when we say we need to control them. When we are controlling something, we are still under the influence of the Kal power.

The way to balance five passions is a continuous repetition of the spiritual **word.** During the sleep hours, the Spirit will take over. We are creating karma all the time, which can be positive or negative. We create karma with every breath we take or what ever we look at. This is the chief cause of karma. We look at something and some passions become active and our minds register our thoughts.

The body follows its dictates. The second cause of creating karma is hearing. So, if we do not see but we can hear, the dictation starts, the body, mind and other faculties become active. The third is speaking. When you see or hear something, you may say something and again, karmas come into action.

This is why all saints and wise men say; 'Silence is golden.'

# FIVE PASSIONS OF THE MIND

The five passions of the mind are as follows.

1.  Kam: lust
2.  Krodh: anger
3.  Lobh: greed
4.  Moha: attachment
5.  Ahankar: vanity

**Kam (lust):** Lust can bring the individual down to the animal level. It is one of the chief passions in this changing world. It is also the principal cause of karma today. Under the influence of Kam, people can create the worst kind of karmas. Even when people know they are creating karma, they do not give a damn about karmic theory. It is such a passion only a few people can stay in balance.

Apart from sexual activities, anything eaten for taste is also lust. Taking drugs, gluttony and abnormal talking are all part of Kam. It is one of the deadliest passions of the mind. Kam is caught mainly by the eyes and heard through the ears and executed through body language. All through history, even up until today, the saints have been influenced by Kam. Temptations are many. During meditation, the saints are influenced by Kal in the form of a beautiful woman.

She can put the saints out of balance. If the saint ignores it and stays calm, he succeeds in his mission. If he gets involved, mentally or physically, the karma has been committed and the mission will fail. This is not the end of him. He can always bounce back by reciting the word. His spiritual vibrations will rise and in this state of consciousness, he will feel the presence of his sister, mum or daughter in that lady.

These are all the stages of unfoldment. Detachment can be the answer. Your love for anything should be pure and above the physical level. Impersonal love is also the answer. The stories and examples on this subject are endless. Find your ways of overcoming this passion. As the yugas changed, the vibrations lowered and the physical organs emerged. During Sat Yuga, the people were not influenced by pleasures.

Being Kali-Yuga, negativity has become so intense that sex nowadays is used mainly for pleasure. This is only the beginning of Kali-Yuga, only about 5,222 years old. The worst is yet to come. Being only 5,222 years old out of 432,000 years, the Kali-Yuga is similar to a newborn baby. 'Can you imagine this baby growing up to be an adult? Try to gain as much spiritual unfoldment as you can and get out of this world into eternity before it is too late. Kam's opposite is chastity (continence).

**Krodh (anger):** Another aspect of the mind keeps the souls trapped in the lower world. This passion can destroy anything in seconds, something you might have achieved over many years. It applies to our relations, built into families, towns and even international. Situations of anger can destroy all that in minutes. A tiny spark is needed to activate this faculty. Nowadays, people are looking for excuses to get angry but most people have little knowledge of karma theory.

The karma theory is not discussed openly in churches or temples and it is not taken very seriously. We see a new wave in today's society, that of the 'angry young man.' The media and movies are responsible for it. They are backing it up by the continuous production of magazines and films. The youngsters feel better if they show their anger. They are unaware of what they are committing.

When we are angry, our sensible thoughts or any soul presence is clouded by dark forces that take control and the destruction of our opponent is inevitable. You want to get on with it and then finish the business there. What has been created in that short period is unexplainable. When the person calms down, he realises he is on the wrong track.

Kal force has a very elusive way of creeping into the individual's mind. It can use any lower four bodies, including astral, causal and mental, to stir up anger, executed by our physical body. Bad dreams can leave their mark for days and stir up anger. The mind is the main instrument for the Kal power but it could be channelled for the Spirit by keeping all five passions in balance.

That way, the actions of the mind fade into the background and the soul body begins to shine. The expression of such a person can be seen on the countenance. Most of these people are awakened souls. Anger indicates defeat in something or failure to express our point to another. If anger comes, let it be for a short period. Make it go away as fast as possible or leave the scene for a while. Sometimes we call it; Timeout.

This will help tremendously; it is called self-control. I don't think anger lets go of anybody. I have seen the Masters get angry. Usually, saints don't get angry but sometimes they pretend to be angry to put the point across to the Seekers. No person can concentrate on meditation as long as they are under the influence of anger. Love is the highest attribute of God, while anger is the lowest attribute of God but one of the highest of Kal.

Being an angry person is not very healthy. The blood thickens and affects the heart slowly and the side effects include heart failure, brain haemorrhage and early death. Some aspects are ill will, evil gossip, fault-finding and jealousy. These are all signs of this aspect. Under the influence of anger, the individual feels like a fire is burning within. Anger is also the element of fire, which is related to the individual's astral or emotional side, binding man to the astral plane. The cure for anger is forgiveness and tolerance.

*Lobh* (**greed**): The whole world is involved in greed. Lots of killings take place to obtain something others have. All robberies that occur in homes, shops or out of people's pockets are influenced by this passion. Nowadays, people use modern technology and computers to do this dirty job. This greed leads from small fights to big wars. If everybody, from households to countries, stayed within their rights and let the rights of others be, there would be no problems.

We do not cross the boundaries of others under these circumstances. 'Who needs to build up walls and borders? The world would be at peace. As they say, 'Charity begins at home.' If we execute this at the domestic level, eventually, it will lead up to the governmental level. Anything we want more than our fair share is greed. Every person who would like to become a millionaire overnight or want something that does not belong to him demonstrates greed. Each must think more about giving than receiving.

The poorest person is the one who will waste his time trying to get something for nothing. Greed often leads to attachment to material things or anger if things don't go your way. Greed attaches the human race to the mineral level, primarily associated with money, gold, silver or property. The cure for lobh is the attainment of contentment. Whatever God has given you is more than enough and you feel you have more than your fair share in life.

**Moha (attachment):** This is another instrument to keep the individual attached to the lower worlds. Nowadays, we have an attachment to everything possible. It is the attachment that we cannot let go of easily. It keeps the individual constantly on the Wheel of Eighty-Four in the lower worlds. It is not very easy to let go of things. Sometimes, we give up a few things but they keep bouncing back to us because the moha is still there in some corner of our minds.

The cure for attachment is the attainment of enlightenment. I have seen many people claiming to be detached from everything when circumstances are normal. When a problem creeps up, which is not even in their close circle, the same people get out of breath, with a dry throat and are lost for words. These are all my practical experiences. It is easier said than done.

I have told Seekers many times when a situation comes up, we know the problem and it is not easy to get rid of it; keep your calm. Half the battle is won. Let the Spirit flow and it will do wonders. The entire battle is won neutrally. Never show your excitement. Then other bodies will also come into action, such as the astral. Every single thing or situation has it's equal and opposite. You only have to look for it.

**Ahankar (vanity):** This is the ego factor in us and is very hard to get rid of; it is often the last to go. It is believed that it can carry on to the next life. The soul body can shake it off only when ready to leave the lower worlds. Mostly, its presence is powerful. Most of the time, we express our ego when we talk to someone to express our point. It is good to feel proud of what we do but this involves the ego. If we don't have it, then the task we are doing seems useless and we don't have the motivation for it.

So, either you do it or you don't, it makes no difference. It's called self-admiration. This faculty of mind executes the mandates of Buddhi, Spirit, in the self's interest. The ego factor has a thousand ways of digging into the minds of the victims. Everyone in this world likes to have a name for themselves and be the centre of attention. Some signs of I-ness are bigotry, displays of wealth, power and bossiness.

All five passions are responsible for creating karma and they are part of the mind. The only way not to create any karma is by always acting in the name of God. Even then, we are creating positive karma. There is no time when we are not creating karma, be it positive or negative, until we go beyond matter, energy, space and time. Remove the shackles of karma, as you are born to be free.

# DREAMS

**The dream state:** Physical life itself is a long dream. At birth, as a child, our dream begins. We daydream and have normal dreams during the night. There are many dreams within the long dream; upon waking, we find ourselves back again, facing the Lord of Karma. If we realise this truth, then many situations we go through in life will not be as painful as we feel. Our realisation tells us, 'Don't worry; It is only a dream.'

We experience horrible dreams and panic so much with fright that we wake up and say, 'Thank God, it was only a dream.' If we are spiritually awake, we can relate our lives to one long dream. We know that we will wake up one day and there will be nothing but happiness. Everyone is not spiritually awake; therefore, we experience many frightening dreams. They affect our minds so much that they can shatter individuals for days.

When any Seeker follows a spiritual Master, the direction of dreams begins to change. The divine dreamer sends forth its dreams via the spiritual Master, arousing the soul in each individual in their sleep to seek the heavenly kingdom of God once more. The Kal sends forth its illusions via negative channels to offset the divine dreams. It is hardly successful, as dreams are part of man's emotional state. The dreams are as real as the actual state of the awakened soul.

Whatever you dream, the dreams are made aware to you via the astral body to the physical senses. Sometimes people are unable to remember what has taken place. There is some weakness in the astral to physical senses but back of our minds, we know that something has taken place. We cannot remember what it was. To clear the doubt, It is not true that we do not dream.

We dream every day; the information we gather during our travels is stored in the subconscious mind. The awakened souls, who are more successful during their spiritual exercises, can go within and seek the required information. You do not have to do any spiritual exercise to gain this information in many cases. There is another little shortcut that I have learned over the years.

Whenever you need some information from the Spirit about something bothering you, contemplate on that problem for a little while and then take a short nap or a few short naps. If it doesn't work on the first or second attempt, try again; it will work. You do not have to lay down or sleep in a bed. Sitting on a sofa or a chair is perfect. During one of these naps, you are guaranteed to get the information you require.

The dream state is as real as the daily daytime experience to some people. Let the Spirit take over. Build yourself up to a state of consciousness where you breathe, eat, work and sleep Spirit. Let the Spirit take over and run your life. Everything will be on automation. Life will be hassle-free and if problems do come, they won't bother you as much.

The problems only occur when we indulge ourselves more in the physical plane than the spiritual. For awakened souls, the problems are there but they are not as strong as they used to be. It is because your spiritual stamina is stronger than your physical. You do not operate from a problem-oriented level of consciousness. You have risen beyond that level, so naturally, problems don't affect or bother you as seriously.

You need to achieve this state of consciousness. You can achieve this state under the guidance of the Master quickly or it may take a lifetime. 'Does it depend on how willing you are to neutralise yourself? I have met many people who want to do it but they often fail regarding the real detachment point. I learned this from my Master when he said many times, 'Use your common sense.'

I have applied this phrase in my life. I am not saying I don't make any mistakes but I make fewer mistakes. Your problems will be minimised, provided you keep your state of consciousness above the lower worlds. It is not worth bringing yourself down to the lower worlds. If you stay positive, you will have fewer problems. Your dream state will also improve. The dreams will be positive and spiritual.

Otherwise, the dreams will be negative with terrifying ghosts, monsters and God knows what. 'Do you know that half of your dreams reflect the daytime thinking process? Which is usually negative. At one time, we almost had direct contact with the Spirit. It was at our disposal, provided by God and through the third-eye. With time, it faded away and we are still lucky to have the dream channel. We can still communicate with the Spirit and feel blessed.

Many people don't believe in or pay attention to the dream state. I wonder if this channel fades away like our third-eye on the physical level. 'What will we do? The Kali-Yuga will grow strong and the dream channel will become inactive. There are three ways of communicating with the Spirit; (**1**) physical, (**2**) dream, (**3**) going within.

1.  The physical approach is inferior and limited.
2.  If we contemplate our problem before going to sleep, then there is a good chance of getting the answers during our sleep. That is, only if you can remember your dream upon waking.
3.  Going within is very rare because not many Seekers are serious about it. People are so busy doing their work that they don't have time. Achieving this state of consciousness is possible but you have to spend a good number of hours or days and sometimes it can take a lifetime. Those who can communicate this way are the superior souls.

**Sleepwalkers:** Sleepwalking is pretty common and many people want to know what happens in this state. The study has shown that 4 percent of people have a sleepwalking disorder, more common in children. The majority of us have experienced at least one episode of sleepwalking. We do get out of this phase of life. Sleepwalking individuals are very deceptive; their eyes are open but their physical senses are shut.

The dream of the experiencer is of a nightmare type. Individuals become so active and strong that they can carry their physical bodies independently. Sometimes, the entity in the dream controls the situation and guides the footsteps of the walker towards a goal of some nature. The person appears to be searching for something or going in a particular direction.

Waking in the middle of a dream and being woken up by someone can be frightening. In some cases, people have died because the entity controlled the individual and unaware of the dangers, walked fearlessly into an accident. In some cases, someone living in a two-storey house and sleeping upstairs began to sleepwalk downstairs to the kitchen area.

They prepared the breakfast and after eating went back upstairs, back to bed and fell asleep. Upon waking in the morning, they had no memory of sleepwalking other than the evidence of the breakfast bowl on the kitchen table. I have been through this experience but I used to take precautions. There is a simple technique that can help.

Before going to bed, take some deep breaths and say to yourself up to ten times, 'I am not going to sleepwalk today. This phrase will be stored in your subconscious mind and if a bad experience occurs, this **command** will neutralise it. You can also improve your dream state by declaring, before going to sleep, I will have good dreams with my spiritual Master.

**Dream within a dream:** It is very strange and rarely happens. I have **experienced** this a few times myself. We go to sleep as usual and begin to dream and during that time, another body wakes up so strongly. It is a higher body than the original dream body. It overpowers the original dream body and sends messages or we become aware of both dreams.

Our astral body passes this memory of both dreams to the physical body when awake. Usually, we wake up after witnessing this kind of experience. We have just seen a very rare vision. Usually, the second dream is from the higher planes.

**Nightmares:** It is pretty common in children and 50–85 percent of the adults report having the occasional nightmare. The nightmares tend to lessen as we age. It is the work of the demon or entities who have stuck with the individual for some time or sometimes indefinitely. They mainly operate in the subconscious body. We catch these entities from negative places such as pubs and clubs.

We are open channels of Spirit and our psychic chakras are open; the entity took the opportunity and entered. During the day, they don't have much effect because we are awake but once we fall asleep, the entity or demon becomes active and begins to do its frightening work. It is terrifying and you sweat and get out of breath. Sometimes, it is so scary that you are scared to sleep again. Some saints can tell the entity not to bother you again.

A true spiritual Master can ward off these entities to leave and not coming back. It happens once you begin to follow the Master and the cloak of the Master is attached to you. When this happens, the demons have no choice but to leave. If you witness someone in the family having a mild nightmare, it is best not to wake them. The only time it's worth waking this person is when a nightmare has a severe effect.

**Blind also dream:** 'Is this dream channel open to everyone? Yes, blindness is only a partial disability. If the person is blinded in later years but before blindness, they saw the world as normal and colourful. The faces they came across in their life will stay in their memory but these faces may never grow old over the years. Their vision will be stuck in the time their blindness occurred. Anyone who has a newborn baby when blinded can only imagine what the child looks like as an adult.

If blindness occurs from birth, the individual will pick up all the sounds but their vision will be imaginary. But in dreams, they can smell, taste, hear sounds, feel, touch and have an emotional feelings similar to any person. They will dream only in black and white. They can also experience nightmares and sleepwalking. Nature always finds its course.

**Past-life dreams:** These are not ordinary dreams. They are only available to a few who have spiritually progressed up to the causal plane; that plane is the past-life storehouse. As you progress to that plane, the book of dreams opens itself to you via the Master's authority.

He will show you the most important past lives, those who have had a significant effect on your present life, especially those on which your present life is based. If you have committed some very bad karma in one of your past lives, you are suffering today. This will justify the answers to your complaints.

**Royal dreams:** In the old days, most of the world was run by kings and queens. These kings were great believers in dream theory. They used to employ experts at explaining dreams in full detail and every morning, they would translate the royal dreams. These interpreters were very gifted people. They could not only interpret but could also see the shortcomings of the future, which were not immediately clear in the dream.

The king used to make his decisions according to dream interpretations. So, if you begin to contemplate on your dreams, they will begin to happen regularly. Start by interpreting them regularly. You will notice that you will find better ways to work them out. To some extent, I can assure you that you can run your life based on your dreams.

**Dream teaching:** This is one of the best methods used by the Master to teach the Seeker. As our physical body is asleep and we wake up spiritually, the Master is ready to teach. The Seeker is taken on spiritual journeys in the dream state but everything seen cannot be remembered. However, the Master can make sure the things you are supposed to remember are correctly stored in your memory upon awakening.

Most likely, he will wake you up instantly so you can grasp it or write it down. Ninety percent of spiritual teachings are given subjectivity and ten percent are given on the physical level through written or verbal material. Dream teachings are easily given and can be given to millions of people simultaneously. It all depends on the capability of the Master.

**Continuity of dreams:** Some of the dreams last the whole night. You have a dream for some reason. You are disturbed by noise or your partner waking you up and trying to fall back to sleep. The dream you were having will continue from where you left off. You may awake again to go to the bathroom and come back and the dream will start again from the point you left off. This has happened to me a few times.

**Prophecy dreams:** This is a very common dream in many people's lives. Some saint appears in your dream and gives you a message of what will happen in your life. Usually, these are near-future happenings. World history is full of prophecy dreams, such as the birth of Jesus and that of many more saints. World leaders receive messages and they act upon them accordingly. My grandmother received the message three days before my birth. I am not claiming to be a saint but it happened. I receive messages about my family and the people I am connected with and they always come true.

I was a fan of Elvis Presley, the singer. I received the message the night before his death, on 16 August 1977. Elvis was on stage playing the guitar, singing and dancing. Although I could see everything he was doing, I could not hear a single word. When I went to work the next day and looked at the newspaper, the headline read, 'Elvis Is No More.' My dream showed me that Elvis would sing no more in simple terms.

# HEART-CHAKRA

It can cause a very frightening experience. It is not a permanent situation. It can only happen when we fall asleep and somehow our hand or part of the arm is placed on top of the heart area. As we sleep, the weight of our hands or arm takes its toll after some time. The heart is trapped and due to that constant weight, it triggers the Heart Chakra to open up psychically.

Although you are sleeping, you will witness many ghostly figures appearing right in front of you and jumping all over your body. They frighten you so much that you wake up in a semi-awakened state. In that state, you cannot move, speak or shout for help and struggle for a long time. The experience will continue until or unless that weight is removed.

Sometimes your partner notices your disturbance and they can remove the hand and the bad experience will terminate there and then. Sometimes, your partner's hand resting on your chest can create the same experience. I have worked out a small technique to get out of this situation but it only works if you can remember it. You need to lift the hand off your chest in a semi-awake state.

**Procedure:** Raise one of your legs six to ten inches high off the flat surface or bed and place it over the other leg. With the strength of the top leg, try to twist your whole body until the hand comes off the heart area. The bad experience will stop there and then. But remember, lifting your leg is not so easy. It becomes heavy because your body is in a semi-paralysed state but I assure you, it can be done.

# DREAM SYMBOLS

I could offer a million dream symbols but still, they would not be enough. The world population is billions and each person experiences the world in their way. Some dreams are like a story, clear and easy to understand but sometimes they appear in symbols that mean the message is hidden. You can try to understand or take advice from the experts or those you trust to reveal the mystery.

I can work around these mysterious symbols reasonably well but sometimes I get stuck with them for a few days. If you contemplate on them, everything will fall into place. The following are some of the common symbols seen in dreams.

**Sea:** This typically represents God due to its calmness. Life depends on water and due to its flexibility, you can beat it or jump into it and remain calm, with no complaints or reactions.

**Child:** This represents Spirit as pure in mind and as innocent as anything.

**Mother:** This symbol indicates protection for the child or anyone.

**Father:** Sometimes, the Master appears as a father figure or guardian angel.

**Eagle:** Soaring in the sky is a sign of freedom.

**Snake:** Being bitten by a snake is always a sign of an impending attack. The number of snakes you see represents the number of people ready to bite you in your life, so be careful.

**Dogs:** A dog barking at you means someone is doing backbiting. The number of dogs represents the number of people. Biting your ankle or hand means that someone is planning to harm you. It also represents entities that may be after you. A dog licking and biting simultaneously means someone is going to bite you in a devious way, someone you trust.

**Tears of blood:** You are going to cry more than usual. You will be hurt so badly you will cry. The loss will be so significant that you may be crying for life.

**Soul upside down:** In your dreams, walking upside down demonstrates that your recent experience comes from the higher worlds. Soul plane and above, for the precise plane of experience, pay attention to the colour of that plane or listen to the sound.

**Sound:** You had the experience but did not remember. All you remember is the sound. It is a hint to indicate the name of the spiritual plane.

**Colour:** Very similar. You don't remember the experience but you do remember the colour. That also indicates the plane you were on.

**Driving a car with no steering wheel:** It shows that you are running your life without proper direction. Sort it out.

**Flying:** This is a sign of soul travel and freedom. If you are flying and you see yourself dropping down like a brick, this could signify danger. We must watch out for the symbols we see in our dreams and if we work around them, we can always know what the dream means.

Once, a Seeker approached me. He was doing reasonably well spiritually but was puzzled by a dream and although it had a positive message, the Seeker, concerned, felt ashamed at what he saw. He said he was flying high in the sky, as free as an eagle but strangely, he noticed his lower half was naked. The Spirit made him aware; all his karmas in the lower worlds were clear.

Once, a lady approached me. I believe once she held a very high state of consciousness but nowadays, she is not up to her previous standards. She said I dream very often when I go to the temple; I lose my shoes or cannot remember where I put them in the first place. Or, when I am going to the temple, I lose my way or go somewhere else.

It indicates she was not what she once was and needed to tune up spiritually. In other words, she was off the spiritual track. Any person can bounce back spiritually and I believe you can too. The chapter on dreams could be infinite, as there is no end to what you can dream. There are many books on the subject available today. Make the most of your dreams, as they are the natural way to communicate with Spirit.

Have good dreams.

# FASTING

Fasting is very much related to spiritual growth. There are two or three different ways of doing it and the most common is not eating food once a week. The other is mental fasting. Stick to one particular day as a discipline not to eat food all day but you may drink water. It is difficult for some people. The next option is to restrict eating to half-day only. Most people can manage this.

Overeating makes people sleepy, which is not healthy for those trying to do meditation and lead a saintly life. Eating very little is not recommended; it can bring down your immune system. Fasting for many days is also not recommended. That is a practice of asceticism. There is another fasting method for some people under the direction of the Master.

You may have the capability to do it and know the reasons behind this. It does not matter how saint you are or how much meditation you do. Certain karmas are not very easy to shake off. Once my Master told me to follow this. Eat the minimum amount of food possible every day, I will say a quarter of your daily caloric intake, just enough for survival purposes.

Do this for forty days at a time and contemplate the situation. You will get the result you are seeking. Some saints guide the Seeker to eat only one grain of rice to materialise results.

'Can you imagine how difficult this would be? It is the last resort to shake off some difficult karmas. I have done with a quarter of my daily intake for sixty days three times in my life. It is a spiritual gain but completely draining of physical energy.

My bodyweight dropped tremendously, I was 80 kg and went down to 65 kg each time and all I could see were bones. With this, you are asking for physical ailments. Some changes came into my physical body, which I didn't like due to this process but there was nothing I could do about it. I will recommend mental fasting because I have tried it and it works wonders.

The procedure is the same; to keep your attention on God, Spirit or Master all day. In other words, all day, your thoughts are spiritual. Once a week and on one particular day, many individuals and religious groups practice on Friday. It does not bother me. You can pick any day most suitable for yourself or your duties. All you have to do is this; From the beginning of the day until you sleep, keep your attention on the subject of God.

Adopt your ways of doing it. You can chant your spiritual word or keep the image of the spiritual Master in your thoughts. If you know any verse from a spiritual book, you can repeat it all day. You can read spiritual material all day or converse with your Master internally. The point is, all day, your theme of thinking is spiritual. I can assure you that it will not be easy in the beginning.

You recite the spiritual word and in no time, you will find your mind is wandering many miles. By the time you discover what is happening, one or two hours may have passed. You may begin the same process repeatedly, keep at it and you will get the hang of it after a while. Now you are on the right track. Most of the time, you can stay on the spiritual subject. Once you have become the Master of it, that is a total success.

Now your mind is trained to keep on the topic of Spirit. Your soul body has become more active and the mind has faded slightly into the background. With this technique, you are not only fasting on Fridays. In effect, you have made a habit of putting your thoughts on God every day.

Now, if you try, you just cannot come off the subject of God. 'Can you imagine your spiritual progress? Now you are doing it daily, continuously repeating the spiritual journey. You have established a permanent connection and talking to your spiritual Master in the inner. Now it does not matter where your Master lives physically, for inner communication distance is no problem.

You are talking to your Master thousands of miles away and the person standing next to you would not have a clue what is happening. The advantage of doing mental fasting is speedy spiritual growth. 'What is a saint? Saints can or believe they can stay in communication with the Spirit all day. 'If you can, then what are you? You will also receive messages from the Spirit or the spiritual fountain within.

What we call **wisdom** keeps pouring itself. You don't have to look for it. If you are looking for something to happen, that is a mental hash bash. When you are mentally neutral, wisdom just appears from nowhere. It appears on your mental screen for you to grasp. It is like water leaking from a cracked ceiling, especially when we are not watching and sitting beneath it.

The water bubble builds up slowly until it drips. The drop comes down on us without warning. We feel the sudden drop on us, feel the sensation and say, 'Wow.' Wisdom appears the same way, especially when we are not expecting it. When you are in tune with the Spirit, wisdom will come daily and sometimes many times a day. This is how the saints wrote most spiritual works.

If the saints sit down and begin to write something, I don't think they write anything spiritual. More or less, they are transcribing thoughts. When we read or hear them, most spiritual writings make us wonder, 'How did they manage to write this? Mind you; they did not create anything from nothing. The 'wisdom' came to them and they managed to write it down on paper.

Fasting without food was challenging for me. My workload consisted of hard manual labour, so I decided to stick with mental fasting. It was a bit difficult but not too hard for me because I enjoyed this inner communication with Spirit and my spiritual Master. I probably met him no more than ten times in thirty years but I never felt far away from him.

I never felt the urge to see him physically because he was always standing in some corner of my house and all I had to do was look for him. 'Can you imagine where this mental fasting can lead you? It is one of the quickest ways to be in the presence of God. Keep it up. One day, you will be surprised to learn that you have done it.

May the Spirit be with you.

# FEELING

A spiritual feeling is a great experience for anyone to have. It does not just happen or create the situation to receive that inner feeling. The person who can receive this inner feeling is most fortunate. It happens by itself when the person is ready to receive the experience. The person should be ready spiritually so the Spirit can pass on the message to them. It is the result of good karma and on that basis, you are a successful spiritual Seeker.

Follow the spiritual Master, who can build up your spiritual stamina to have this experience. It may take a few months or take up to a few years. It depends on how prepared you are to receive this inner feeling, which is a live experience and definitely not something you can make or believe. That will be false and have no value whatsoever. I followed the Master for about a year and walked up and down Southall Broadway with a fellow Seeker, displaying meeting posters in shop windows.

Some shopkeepers were friendly, while others were not. One day, suddenly, I felt something within myself. As we were approaching a shop to ask the business owner if we could display our poster in the window, each time, I received a powerful feeling within which told me very clearly, 'Do it. It will be all right' or 'Don't do it. It is not going to work in this shop.' I was surprised. I said to myself; Gosh, I don't believe it, I am getting the answers in advance!

My friend was a very nice person but not a very good listener. If we had decided to go in any shop, at the same time, I got the inner message, 'Go ahead. It is going to be okay.' After a few shops, I got the message; Your poster will not be accepted this time. I told my friend, 'This time, it is not going to be accepted,' but stubbornly, he turned around and said, 'No, we will do it.'

The result was that we failed. I told him, 'I told you it was not going to work.' He was surprised that I was correct every time I told him in advance. I never told him that I am an open channel for Spirit. Since that day, it has remained with me and it has been a great help. One more thing to be careful about; When you receive an inner feeling, catch it straight away and act upon its instructions. It works.

If you receive the feelings and delay the action or doubt it, it will not work. You have diluted that feeling with delay and doubt and it loses its spiritual power. So, it would help if you acted instantly. The more you follow, the clear the message will be. Trust the Spirit within. There is no better guide than the Spirit itself. 'If Spirit is working for you, why do you have to use your impaired judgement?

You don't have to see God. Nobody can see God apart from a very few but God has many ways of showing its presence to genuine Seekers. All we have to do is make ourselves available to receive its presence. God is everywhere, within you and in all your surroundings. There is not a single iota where it is not. Only we are off the track and travelling in the opposite direction. God is everywhere for us to experience.

# PATIENCE

You will be surprised to learn this is one of the key points behind spiritual success. In other fields, such as work, politics, business or sports, you can apply a level of aggression and be successful. As far as spiritual success is concerned, you cannot use any aggressiveness. If you do, you will go back to square one. Patience is the key to your spiritual success. It does not happen overnight. It may take a few months or years.

It depends on you finding the right person to lead you. My present Master has given us spiritual exercises, which he recommends that we practice every day. Some people who did not follow any Master decided to leave their homes and meditate in the Himalayan mountains. During winter, the temperatures are sub-zero. Concentrating on the spiritual eye and creating an image to ponder upon requires a lot of patience.

In such a case, if success does not happen, it leads to lots of frustration leading to broken discipline. Patience is the key factor to building discipline and overpowering frustration. Broken discipline and frustration are the channels of the negative force. We can overcome these negative traits if we have patience. Patience can lead us to have nobility, which has the qualities of goodwill, love for all and kindness.

These traits reflect on your countenance. They will also lead to self-mastery, allowing one to do great things on humanitarian grounds. But without patience, you cannot self-surrender to the Master. With self-control, you will become as calm as the sea and not resist evil. You cannot win evil by fighting against it. Evil will try all the tricks in the book to make you break your discipline; it will make you aggressive or impatient because you have had no success.

Impatience leads to destruction. All the problems we have as individuals, families and nations result from impatience. Everyone keeps their fingers on the trigger. 'Have we ever seen any fruitful achievements come out of this? The answer is destruction, mentally or on an international scale. We are the children of God but are running wild, without any goal or good cause.

However, we are fully trained in negative traits, such as telling lies, backbiting, fighting, displaying our superiority over others, creating enemies and being an enemy.

We still portray ourselves as serious believers in God by doing all this. 'Are we really? We are not doing our homework to find out who we are. Some people I know have been trying to bring about my downfall for years. They have tried everything possible.

I, knowing every action of theirs, did not react. I leave all in the hands of the Spirit. The people involved will reap what they sow. Patience is one of the main attributes of God. God is the most patient. All souls are part of the great body of God, like all the particles assembled become soil or all the drops put together to become the ocean. If some atoms of the great body are causing disruption, 'Does God get angry and serve punishment to teach you or me a lesson? The answer is no.

It lets you be and allows you to move on to the next step because it knows, one day, you will know too. The mind is the key player in misleading. In Kali-Yuga, the mind is the king and the soul stays in the shadow or in the background. It has no say. The mind is not supposed to be patient. It has the quality of mischief. It cannot sit still and focus on one point like a monkey, growing frustrated if stopped.

It takes lots of patience to control the mind to awaken the soul body so it can take the driver's seat. Once the soul is awake, the mind itself will fade into the background. All souls are created equal, we are made from the spark of God and we have its qualities. If there is any difference between us as humans, it is the fact that we are operating at different states of consciousness, according to our unfoldment.

As God has patience with all its creation, we should have too. We all have our own psychic space and must give others too. Without patience, nothing is possible. 'Our goal is of high, become yea calm as sea and wise as an old tree with patience, you will be close to thee.'

Patience, calm, calm, patience.

# PURITY

Spirit is pure and it is your goal to be as pure as Spirit. God dwells within those who are pure in their hearts. God is everywhere but it has unique places where it feels more comfortable. These are the people who are open channels for the Spirit and God can express itself freely and convey its message to the people. We notice that some people are an expression of God. People comment; yes, God speaks through this person and usually, we call them saints.

These saints have faced many struggles against the odds in this world. Forget about purifying yourself for a minute. Breaking out of any religious system you have been raised in is another challenge. It would help if you kept striving towards your goal and this should be your primary mission; to have God-realisation in this life. It will only happen when you have closed all the other avenues of life, which are many and now have only one avenue open. That is to be the available channel for the Spirit.

At this moment, all other mental occupations have gone to the side, God dwells within and purity is achieved. Purity is always a positive element. It is a continuous process until the end of your life on Earth and it will continue above too, so you may become an assistant with God. We do not have to act like little children but we must become like little children. It is an expression of attitude, which should be honest and innocent.

Look closely into the eyes of a newborn child. You can see the expression of Spirit as a symbol. A child in your dreams represents Spirit. When a child is born in any family, we tell that child into which system they are born and we lead the way for them to follow. When these children come to their senses, finding out where they are and who they are, it is far too late to reverse time. Then the individual makes all the plans to break out of the religious system.

It takes a lifetime to get out of a system we were not supposed to be. We are lucky if we can manage to break out of any system in a single lifetime. The shackles of karma keep children tied to the ground on which they are born. As we are born in the lower worlds and then fully trained to be negative, we are negative, so the result is hopeless.

We are forced to lose some of the purity we were born with, realistically speaking.

Build your inner temple upon a foundation of purity. Whatever is in your heart will reflect on your countenance. The outer follows the inner, so always prepare yourself for the inner and the outer will follow automatically. Inner purity will lead us to God and those who are pure in their hearts will reflect God in their expressions. These are the people who are very near and dear to God.

The inner house built on a negative foundation will lead you to such a mess that it will be difficult to get out. Ghosts, devils and drunk entities will enjoy your company. I am sure they need to stay somewhere too but they have more places than they bargained for. Every house around the corner is available and they can walk in with no struggle.

'Is this purity of physical, mind or soul body? It is pure overall. To some extent, physical purity is necessary. The purity of the mind is the most important. The soul itself is pure but the purity of the soul is required for you to unfold and gain as much awareness as possible. It is the soul's achievement to become an assistant with God, as the mind and physical body are temporary tools to be used as required in the lower worlds.

Those who want to stand on spiritual grounds must stay put. We have to guard ourselves and must not let a single iota of negative thoughts enter our system, the one for which we have worked very hard. You have achieved purity and can maintain it. God-realisation is yours to have. It is a state of consciousness that no one can deny.

God is not tied to any dos' or don'ts; however, maintaining the purity of the Master' picture and holy scriptures is also very important. Pure Spirit is subtle. Listen and act upon it. It leads you to God and you will not be disappointed.

God loves those who are pure in their hearts.

# HARMONY

Harmony must be an essential factor in our lives. Wherever harmony is, peace is guaranteed. Harmony means that we agree with our doings; it may be in the family or office, especially on the spiritual path. It is the backbone of our success. Upon discussion, if one member does not agree, the meaning of a meeting or Satsang is lost. It is the negative vibrations of a person that can bring forth negative results.

Without harmony, people will not feel the positive vibrations they came to experience, especially newcomers. When a person is in harmony, we see the spiritual glow on their faces. You do not have to utter a single word; people around you will feel the spiritual vibrations. We can help the world be a better place with this harmonised spiritual atmosphere. It works when we say we do this for the 'good of the whole,' it works. This is how we become the assistants of the Master.

All world problems today result from a lack of harmony with one another. If someone does not agree, he should step aside and let others do the job. It is much better than creating negativity. Avoid negativity and let the Spirit do its miracles. This is the main problem today; everyone wants to be superior to others, be more powerful and dominant. It is important to get rid of your ego, the destroyer of peace.

If we stay within our rights and try not to grab anything from others or harm anyone else, we are in harmony with ourselves and others. Peace is accomplished. If we take this to a large scale, such as countries and the world, we will not require any boundaries or borders. If we stay within our limits and within our circles, we will not need any police or government to interfere. Everyone will live in peace and the whole world will be a better place to exist.

The flow of Spirit will be more significant and humanity's spiritual unfoldment will be better. To create this harmony, you have to become harmonised within yourself. It comes by doing everything with discipline. Do your spiritual exercises, practice the presence of the spiritual Master and do everything in the name of God. You are just the channel for the Spirit.

When you come to this state of consciousness, you will not want to interfere with anyone or anything around you. It does not matter, whatever it may be. Harmony is accomplished. You must be an example to others. Those people who create disharmony create much negative karma. Instead of gaining spiritual ground, we begin to lose it and the flow of Spirit is not as strong as it used to be.

May peace be with you.

# THE TEMPLE OR FIRE WITHIN?

The teachings we follow must lead us to the temple within; if not, we should work on our success or failure points. A few months of complete sincerity are enough to lead a peaceful life. The fire within does not let us settle mentally to observe any solid experience. This fire within is based on fear, worry, jealousy, greed and attachment. Most likely, our mind is occupied by one of these factors or a few at a time.

These factors affect us badly, especially when sitting alone and having nothing else to do. The unoccupied mind is taken over by negative thoughts based on the negative factors we are going through. We have built lots of negativity around us and we are the victims of it. There is always someone in the family who makes you feel uncomfortable in their presence. When that person enters the house, a shiver runs up your spine.

It is the fear that makes you sit uncomfortably in your meditation. Your thoughts are, 'Now what will happen? or 'Will this person find out what I am doing? 'How can you succeed when all this is going on within you? Do not fear; nothing will happen. It is the creation within; these are the creatures of fire. Greed will also make you wonder how to achieve something on a material basis.

Your mind is busy all day making further plans. All your thoughts are destructive and nothing is progressive, whereby you can gain some spiritual ground. Greed can turn into jealousy if someone else is striving for the same goal and you don't want to let them win. Your thoughts are on how to bring the other person down. You will plan deceptions; it is going on in most families.

There is always someone in the family who is doing better than you and you cannot tolerate their success. You will do everything to bring them down from their throne. Very rarely do people help or are happy with their success. When loved ones are helpless, they will try to bring you down to their level. I have seen them consult black magicians to help. Jealousy can destroy you.

You will try to harm your loved ones and to some extent, you will be successful. The harm you have done to yourself may take a few lifetimes to recover. We have this battleground going on within ourselves all the time without us realising it. We are supposed to be doing meditation but we become wanderers in thought as soon as we sit down. We travel to India, China, Japan and New York.

We should contemplate meeting the Master to see the light or hear the sound. We should be in a particular mood to do our meditation. Our minds should be calm. Once the mind is overactive, it will not let you sit still. You can meditate anytime you wish if you are relaxed and tuned into the Spirit. I suggest doing your spiritual exercises early in the morning when the mind is not fully awake and the noise level is also minimal.

Success does not depend on how long you sit. It depends on the success of your sitting. All negative thoughts will destroy whatever you are trying to achieve. Some people are peaceful, sincere followers but are driven up the wall by others who are jealous. In this situation, you are about to attack them in your thoughts. That is deadly during spiritual exercise.

You can harm the other person badly. This level of anger can lead to your ill health. We become sick first, which destroys the positivity within us most of the time. The vibrations we carry are at their lowest and the flow into the body cells is negative, so they become unhealthy, which leads to a physical breakdown. Anger is responsible for thickening our blood, leading to heart attacks.

Worry and fear lead the person into depression and become mentally sick. We cannot imagine what is going on within us. If we follow our teachings sincerely and execute the Master's instructions step by step, we can overcome all these negative traits and become calm internally. We need to replace all the junk with pure Spirit, which will lead us to have a positive attitude, positive thinking and a pure channel for Spirit.

Once you have done that, your outer will follow the inner. Now the temple within is ready. If the temple within is occupied with these creatures of fire, there is no room for the Master or the Spirit to reside and there will be no spiritual success. It does not matter how hard you try and how good your Master is. It is the fight within.

Give yourself a fresh start. Success will be yours.

# ILLUSION/MAYA

Illusion is a veil that hides reality. Maya obstructs the ways of the spiritual Seeker. It is one of the main tools used by the negative force. There are millions of ways it can deceive the Seeker. Most Seekers believe they are seeking God but actually are seeking illusion. Anything that is attracted to your mind is an illusion. Excitement is the main attraction. The attraction is to amuse the senses with psychic powers.

Everyone is interested in creating something that will impress others to show them we are superior. We have a vision as a Seeker. If we analyse it thoroughly, we conclude that most of our seeking is Maya. Any experience on the physical plane that ends up on the mental plane is an illusion. The spiritual Master can guide the Seeker on how to avoid illusion successfully. The physical plane is a living example of illusion.

Whatever you do, think, create or work for is an illusion. Whatever we live and die for is an illusion. Anything you can think of which is not permanent is all illusion. Whatever we see is an illusion. Whatever unseen is reality hiding in disguise. This is why you cannot see Spirit; because it is permanent. Our eyes are part of the illusion, this is why the light and sound are beyond their reach.

We can see the light or hear the sound when our senses are open to higher vibrations. This happens during meditation or our thoughts are on the spiritual side. When Seeker steps onto the path of reality, he faces illusion at every step of life. Sometimes, the Master himself creates illusory situations to test the Seeker. The Master watches patiently for the Seeker to recognise the illusion and pass with full marks.

If Seeker succeeds in his efforts, the Master is happier than the Seeker himself. If Seeker is struggling, a helping hand is just around the corner. The Master does want the Seekers to pass with their efforts; otherwise, the Seekers will not be as strong spiritually as the Master expects them to be. But the Master has all the patience in the world.

According to the teachings, if the Seeker is doing fine, the negative force steps in to bring about the downfall. Kal is not very happy for the Seeker if their soul leaves this world. Every person is a slave to the dictates of Kal. We put our full attention on material gains, especially money; we expect it to appear at every corner. If we direct our attention toward God with the same strength, it will appear more quaker.

'Do you know why? Because God is available at every corner, in any direction you look. It is waiting for you to make the gentle approach and experience its presence. Kal is more of a clever type. The more you seek, the more it gets away from you. Money, gold and diamonds are part of the illusion scheme to make you run wildly after them. Only a few will catch them; the rest are driven insane. The physical life ends and you never achieved enough to become satisfied and you are a successful slave to Kal.

Kal does show some illusory insights to keep you in its grip. Sometimes, Kal can take the form of your Master and appears to you to give you some deceiving message. It can use you as a channel to pass on the message to your fellow Seekers. The Master never uses anyone as a middle person to convey his message. He always appears to the Seeker directly to give guidance. Under these circumstances, the pseudo-master must be challenged.

Say, 'In the name of God, are you the Master? If the appeared Master is true, he will stay and give spiritual discourse or whatever message he has come to share. If it were the creation of illusion, then he would vanish instantly. Those seeking God but not having a living Master are totally under deception. The negative entities appear and show them some vision to keep them under control. The Seeker believes that he is directly connected with God.

Many Seekers are mentally disturbed and are under the control of an entity that uses individuals to satisfy itself and gives false messages. People believe this fellow is a saint when, in fact, he is suffering from depression. Under these circumstances, the person needs medical help. True saints do not create drama. Their approach to spreading the message is subtle. Most seekers would not realise that he is around.

A few times such illusive situations were created before me. Known faces were used to make everything appear to look real. Once, I was so impressed with the situation that I had no doubt it was real. When I investigated further, everything vanished into thin air. Maya is capable of creating scenes that look like paradise. This usually takes place on the astral plane. New scenery is created with new footpaths to lead the Seeker in the wrong direction.

The police on this plane are also watchful for new arrivals, those wandering around but don't have any kind of protection. They catch, control and play with them as they please. Sometimes the planter and the planted and the experiencer are the same people. This illusion takes place during the process of imagination. The Master creates this illusion every day to test the Seeker. The Master is working on the weakness of the Seeker.

The Seeker is aware of what he is working on and once he feels that he has worked off any of his weaknesses, he has passed the test. For example, money. In your dream, the Master will disguise himself and offer you an amount of money you have never seen before. If you accept it, you have failed. If you say, 'This is no longer of any use to me,' then you have passed and the Master might appear in his proper form and bless you.

The weaknesses are all related to the five passions of the mind. If your weakness is Kam (lust), the Master will create the illusion of a beautiful lady or a handsome man and test you accordingly. If you are an angry person, he will create a situation to test your patience. If you have lost your temper, that means you have failed. If not, you have succeeded. It is the same with moha (attachment). The illusion will show that you have lost the most loved one or material item; the Master watches your reaction to your loss.

Whether you pass or fail depends on your spiritual stamina. Ahankar (vanity) is the last to go. The Master might create the situation to see if you have conquered your ego. As you can see, the Master creates the illusion for your benefit. Most of them are for testing and many are created to alert you. When the negative force creates an illusion, it is to mislead you. There are no complex or easy rules you have to pass the first time.

There is always a second or third chance. As long as the Master knows that you are making an effort, he will make sure you pass successfully. The Master has taken the responsibility of making you the Master of your universe. As we follow the spiritual path and achieve our spiritual success, we go through thirty-two facets of experiences.

We can perform many miracles when we do this but the Master keeps them under control because most facets are related to illusion. The Master does not want you to get attached to any one of them; otherwise, you may lose the purpose of your seeking. The attractions are many and the mind is ready to get involved in any one of them.

The illusion is part of a soul's journey into the lower worlds and illusion leaves the soul on its leaving the lower worlds for good. Illusion has been created purposely in the lower worlds to entangle the soul into a web. Kal creates attractive situations to educate the souls. At the end of its journey, the soul has learned enough and can differentiate between illusion and reality and it is free to leave forever.

Reality is. All else is an illusion.

# WHAT IS TELEPATHY?

Telepathy is mental communication from one person to another, silently, without verbal language. It can happen naturally or you may have experienced this communication a few times. For example, you heard someone call you from nowhere, yet you know the person's voice. Upon communication with the person in concern, 'Do you know, I heard you call my name at a certain time? The answer is, 'Yes, I was thinking of you at that time.'

The reason for the hearing is; the strength of that person's thoughts at that particular time. It proves that his mind was focused on you without any interference. The thoughts must be one-pointed and this is what we have to learn if we are going to adopt the art of telepathy. It is not much of a gain according to actual spiritual heights. Most people are interested in the field of telepathy.

It is a basic and temporary achievement but to keep communication alive, it must be practiced regularly or it will fade away after some time. A single person cannot practice as you send the messages to someone. When the other person is not aware of what is taking place, there will be no response, as it has been a one-sided approach. Sometimes this happens naturally between two people, as they are so close to each other mentally and psychically.

Two people have to decide and practice at the agreed time of the day. It will be much easier if you are in the same house but in separate rooms, so the communication contents can be discussed or exchanged easily. First, you must meditate for a few minutes to clear your mind from wandering thoughts. To begin the practice, sit in separate rooms and use short sentences, such as 'God is one' or any other which is your favourite.

Do not tell each other what words you will use; otherwise, your imagination will begin to play about and it will not be true communication. You must hear something out of the blue that you do not expect. Do practice daily. You will have success in a short period. Once this communication is established between two people, distance is no problem.

You can communicate whenever or wherever you like. Once you have learned it and know how to do it, you can always bounce back. The saints always use silent language to communicate because it is more effective, pure and effortless. As the knower of telepathy, you become more receptive to deja-vu and ESP.

# INITIATIONS / DIKHSHA

Initiation is a link to admitting someone into spiritual society. During the second initiation, Master links the Seeker to light and sound. It is the most significant step for the Seeker on a spiritual journey. Without this process, the spiritual journey of the Seeker will be at a standstill. You need a living Master who can work on both sides of the spiritual world to do this. That is inner and outer Master.

The Seeker should be spiritually ready to be connected to the light and sound. The initiation will not be given on the first meeting between the Master and the Seeker. A spiritual foundation is very important to receive the blessings of God. I don't think we can build a good house on shaky grounds. The Seeker receives the first initiation in the dream state, given within the first year of joining.

It is the first step indicating the acceptance of the Seeker by the Master. The second initiation is the most important step for the Seeker. The approximate time expected for this is a minimum of two years. The reason for this is to build a good spiritual foundation. The Seeker has studied and has learned the fundamental truths of the teachings. It is decision time for the Seekers if the path is suitable for them.

Once the Seeker has decided to go ahead, there is no looking back. The Master initiates you personally or this is done by one of his appointees. Spiritually, it makes no difference.

During this process, the Master is present physically, if not spiritually. The Seeker has received the link to Spirit; it will help travel within the inner planes. This is also your connection to communicate with the spiritual Master.

Your journey has begun. There is not a hairbreadth between the Master and the Seeker. I have had this experience myself living in England. My Master was living in America and we communicated daily. It is all possible if you are linked to light and sound. You will experience the Spirit and the spiritual Master as close as your heartbeat.

'Who wants to write letters or make phone calls if you have this kind of communication? Initiation is a spiritual ritual similar to 'Amrit' in Sikhism and baptism by Christians. Other religions in this world perform this ritual in different manners. If the followers feel that they have been connected to the light and sound, that is well and good but being the recipient, you must analyse the initiator performing this ritual on you.

'Are they capable of doing it? If you want this initiation because others are getting it or someone has talked you into it, I don't think you will go very far spiritually. Being initiated is a solemn responsibility. It requires your total commitment and life will not be as easy as you might expect. It is going to be tough. You want the spiritual experience and the Master will ensure you get it.

Balancing your karma will be speeded up and demanding situations will spring up like weeds that have never been seen or heard of before. Most of them will be from your previous lives, which must be cleared to achieve the next step. The sooner you go through them, the better off you will be.

The initiations mean nothing if you do not live up to that state of consciousness. When the initiation was given, you were ready for it.

If you do not maintain that state of consciousness, you will drop like a solid rock. Once you have received the light and sound initiation, you cannot leave spiritually. The Spirit will not leave you. The most important initiation is soul initiation, which results in Self-realisation and finally God-realisation. You have become the Master of your universe and the Master has a new co-worker to assist him spiritually and physically.

The initiations above (God-realisation) are for
the Masters only.

# LIVING IN THE PRESENT MOMENT

The present moment is the king, all else is an illusion and nothing is more precious than the present moment. It just is. All eternity is in this moment. At one time, we lived in this moment. Long ago, this was the situation when people did not discuss what time, day, week, month or year it was. It was the same with counting numbers, one to a hundred. Nowadays, we count millions, billions and beyond.

When I was young, during1960s, people used to count up to twenty and then repeat twenty in my part of the world and finally, they said; I bought this item for this many twenties. Figures such as hundreds and thousands were available in maths only. 'How many people had watches? Maybe one in a thousand. In those days, most people were living in the present moment. They had a tremendous love for all life and were at peace within.

Since time has become more of a factor, we live in the past or dream about the future. We rarely live in the present moment because something is always bothering us. Education is good but in fact, it is taking you away from yourself and one day, you will not know who you are. The nearest description of yourself will be 'robot.' How peaceful would it be if we only knew that today would be the last.

'What is the time? It is only a part of the education system. 'What is on the clock? It is the present moment, which is continuously moving. What has gone behind the clock is known as the past and what will take place will be our future. Life is a continuous succession of 'now' or continuity of 'is-ness.' Is or now is also on the continuous move, so we cannot hold any is or now in our grip and stop it from moving.

It will never happen; otherwise, the day and night will not happen. All eternity will be in a mode of suspension. The makers of time won't be able to move. The changes in the lower worlds will not happen. The time-track theory will not work. We have to learn the theory of time collapsing. Nothing is going to stop for any one person or us. Everything is moving and will continue to move or we will have no winter, summer, autumn or spring.

This is created for the lower worlds to breathe. So, 'What is going to move or stop? It is us. We have to learn how to suspend our state of consciousness. While it is in suspension, you are living in the state of bliss, which you may call a continuation of the present moment. You will not be bothered by how many 'now's have come and gone in this state of consciousness. In the present moment, nothing matters.

Problems are based on the past or the future. Karmas are based on the past and the future. They are also based on the present if you are creating them. Those who act in the name of God or live in an eternal bliss state do not create negative karma, only positive karma. The statement 'We do not create karma' is incorrect, as we create karma, either positive or negative. This is the spiritual law in the lower world.

If we learn how to live in the present moment, 'Will we care what will happen tomorrow or what happened yesterday? As you have done nothing wrong, in return, nothing can touch you. If you have done something wrong, it will disturb you at this moment. It all depends on the state of consciousness you are carrying. Those who live in the present moment do not win or lose, happy or sad.

In this state, you can give, while in the past, you received. The one who gives is the prince and the one who receives is the pauper. Now you see the strength of the present moment. In the worlds of Kal, there is past and future, day and night, happiness and sorrow. This is the game you are trapped in; reality lives in the present moment. If you want to have God in your life, you have to decide and act now.

Self or God-realisation is not a game. You decided to open up to the Spirit. It may not happen in one day, one month or a year. If your decision is final, it will not be long to experience the bliss state. Now you are in the driving seat, whereas before, you were a passenger in the transport of Kal and it led you nowhere. In the present moment, you are part of God and it is part of you and the fragrance of God is reaching out to others through you. Nothing is more precious than the present moment. It just is.

This is your shining eternal life via Spirit. Every word you speak is about God and it should be as if God is speaking through you and is expressing itself to others. Those who listen to your words of wisdom should feel blessed. Those who are not feeling well should be healed. Those who are at unease should have peace. Those who want to feel the presence of God should do so. For those who want anything, the world should be theirs to have.

This must be your goodwill. When you see, you should see only God. Every creation of this world is an expression of God in different forms. As you see, every particle is God; you should know that it is itself. You should feel the presence of God as you see every expression of it. The world is yours to see. You are on top of the world and you are within the world. You are the world, the universe, universes and all in yourself.

Every breath you take should be like the sound on a continuous circle to and from God. You travel on it as you go and experience and come back. It is continuous and everlasting for all of creation. Every taken breath, in or out, should be as if you are communicating with God. The number of breaths taken in or out are not many. Make sure you have used them wisely. 'Breathe in and breathe out is the secret. The world is lying right in front of you. It is yours to have and experience.

Whatever you hear should be the word of God, the music of the spheres. The message of God should be for the good of the whole. It could be a whisper. It could be a little click. It could be the thunder. It could be running water or the buzzing of the bees or sweet violin or the flute's melody. Nothing else should enter the horizon. It is the sound and sound itself.

Every action should be in the name of God. Every jerk in the body should move with the naam (word). Every step you take should be in the naam, from left foot to the right and from right foot to the left. The steps are not many. Take them wisely. Don't waste any step, breath, sound, word or sight. It is a privilege to see and feel all, as you are the one and it is the one and we are the one. Action is yours and the reaction is also yours.

Every action is positive. Those who come your way will also be positive. May the positives be and all the blessings be.

You have suspended eternity in your universe. Those who live in this state of consciousness are Self or God-realised. It depends on their success in continuously maintaining their attention, moment to moment.

This continuous effort will lead them to Self or God-realisation with the help of inner and outer teachings of the Master. The task seems vast but once you have mastered it, as the swimmer swims with ease, you will be like the wise old tree and calm as the sea. No weather bothers the wise old tree or the calm sea.

In the present moment–just be.

# LOVE

Without love, nothing can exist. God's love for its creation makes everything in existence possible. Without this great love, everything would turn into dust. This love flows from the Ocean of Love and Mercy through the spiritual worlds and down to Earth. It touches every atom in existence and even those that are not in reality, as they are still dwelling in the seed worlds.

One drop from the ocean can be divided into millions of small particles. There is no place where God does not exist. Without its love, nothing would move or grow. With this love, we are having our being in it. We live on this love. We breathe, see, hear or eat and the list is endless. Love is the primary communication between God and its creation. The means of communication is Spirit, one of its main attributes.

'What is Spirit? It is pure love. It is the combined force of light and sound. With the medium of divine light and sound, we can communicate successfully. Light is knowledge; the ability to see all the pitfalls on our travels and sound is a vehicle we can travel. Sound is the way to our wonderland. Everything you see is light. Different shades of colour express their vibrations and are bonded by the sound.

All the noises we hear are sounds and are expressed individually according to the different levels of vibrations. Pure Spirit is the greatest love. No other love is superior to this. The love we express in the physical world is not pure. It has different values. It depends on our expression. The love between two people, as husband and wife, is not pure. It is an expression of attraction to each other. The love expressed through a sexual union is not pure. It is most likely lust.

Love of our children is more of a need in our lives and mostly, it is attachment. We demonstrate our love to receive love. Otherwise, we feel like a broken branch on the tree, drying away the moment to moment. Love, in a sense, is another desire to survive. We must love unconditionally. No love is pure in the lower worlds. You cannot love everyone, only a few nearest relations but you can always give impersonal love to everyone who comes your way.

Love thy neighbour as thyself; there is no room for hatred. You must give love to receive love and fill yourself with so much love that it flows out of you to touch others. I love all its creations, animals, birds, insects, minerals, flowers, plants and trees. You cannot afford to have the slightest negative feelings that can change the course of your life. No one can see God or become God. It is one and only one.

It just is but its presence and expression are present in every corner of this universe and beyond. If you cannot feel its expression through a blade of grass or the fragrance of a flower or the flow of love in the eyes of a child who is as innocent as itself, then you must be a dull person in this field. God is here and everywhere for you to see and feel. Everything you see or feel has been created for you to remind you of its existence.

We all take this love of God for granted and refer to it as nothing. People who claim there is no God need to open up until the truth expresses itself. Pure love flows from the Ocean of Love and Mercy. You will feel wonderful and wanted by itself as an assistant.

Love all as it loves you.

# MIRACLES

This is one of the most loved topics of all religious followers. It does not matter what teachings they follow. Once they hear the word **miracle,** they become alert and pay attention. Without seeing any miracle, the average follower will lose faith in the teachings. They probably walk away to seek other teachings to fulfil their desires. Once you know the teachings you follow are genuine and will lead you to your destiny, you will not be interested in miracles because your faith will carry you through to your goal.

If you do not see any miracles, your faith must be rock solid. If you have that, you are a true follower and success will be yours. If you do not see any miracle, you are expecting and feel discouraged, you need to work on your spiritual foundation. Some leaders show miracles to attract the Seekers; you will find that these people are tricksters, not saints. As far as your spiritual progress is concerned, that will be nil.

The spiritual knowledge given to us by God is free and it must be distributed free to worthy souls. There may be a small charge (donation) to help run the distribution department and mailing cost; that is reasonable. God does not live or breathe in big organisations. This way, we lose the entire purpose of the teachings. If you examine it closely, you will find that life itself is a miracle. The true miracle is changed consciousness, which results from going within and following spiritual instructions.

The true Master always leads you to the inner. Miracles seen on the outer are just to satisfy the mind. In other words, it is mental food but it helps to build up the faith too. A loss of confidence will lead you nowhere. Overindulgence in seeing miracles will also lead you nowhere. Once the miracles stop, you will lose interest and never be heard of. In the first instance, you may be only attracted to the teachings to see the miracles you heard from others.

Miracles do take place but of their own accord. No one can force miracles to happen. The Master appears to you during meditation or in your dream state to take you on the spiritual journey or you can receive spiritual wisdom. Sometimes he appears as light or a little touch on your shoulder when you know that no one is around or hear different sounds. Sometimes you notice him smiling in one of the pictures displayed in your room.

He appears to you in the street but in disguise or you do not see him but you feel his presence. Or, after appearing to you in the street, he may disappear into the crowd without a trace. The Master appears in many ways but he always appears when we do not expect it. Those who see him frequently are blessed. Many miracles occur during your Satsang, as this is a live experience for some. You are awake during Satsang and will see the Master standing in the middle of the group.

The image of your teacher disappears and in his place, the Master himself is sitting. The teacher is blessed as the Master expresses that he is taking the Satsang and you are also blessed to witness it. The same happens during spiritual meetings. Spiritual chants are generally performed with the eyes closed but the Master opens your eyes so you can witness his presence or give you some special message.

Numerous miracles occur at your workplace or during your child's birth or at someone's funeral. Personal experiences happen during your spiritual exercise as you see the light or hear the sound. Or the Master appears at your third-eye or during soul travel. Or you see yourself on the ceiling and sitting on the floor, doing meditation. The Masters appear in their spiritual bodies in your room where you meditate.

I have seen all these experiences myself and I know many of you have seen them numerous times. 'What more do you want to see? All these situations lead to one point. The Master is present as he says, 'I am always with you.' Even one of these experiences is good enough to lead you through this life. It does not matter how much you see. An unstable mind will never be satisfied.

It wants to see something during every meditation sitting. Most likely, you are looking for dramatic experiences to wander around like a toy. If you have these out-of-body experiences, 'How far can you go? 'Maybe visit your relatives or scare someone? These are all mental requirements. External experiences always relate to travel and with the word travel, you cannot go further than the etheric plane.

The real meaning of soul travel is a change of consciousness, which relates to the inner planes. The Master makes sure that you are not a wandering soul and he does make sure you will be shown and given experiences based on your requirements; no more than that. Excessive power in untrained hands leads to destruction. Misused power during anger against anyone destroys the opponent and yourself as well.

You have to learn how to raise your vibrations with discipline. The Master is always waiting at the Sun and Moon worlds. To have a glimpse, you have to raise your vibrations. When you see the Master during Satsang or spiritual chants, your vibrations make it possible to have a glimpse. Sometimes, Master himself raises your vibrations to give you the experience.

You are the creator of all miracles. Keep your state of consciousness high and you will see miracles in every corner of your life. Keep this channel open. Do not let the negative Spirit block it. A blocked channel will not let the pure Spirit flow and the result will be a negative experience and frustration as a whole or maybe a loss of faith. You must learn to bounce back if you feel negative, which is also a miracle.

The Master himself is a miracle. You, as his representative, are also the channel for miracles. The Master shows the miracles to the requirement and uses you to express them. Many advanced Seekers are being used but the Spirit is always in command. I can assure you, in this lifetime, you will see enough miracles. Then you will say, 'Yes, I have seen enough.' Our mind is very clever but sometimes it has a very short memory.

Always write down your experiences, including the dates and times; pick up your book and read whenever you are feeling down. It will give you extraordinary power and you will bounce back to normal. Your vibrations have changed and your faith in the Master and in his teachings is restored. Miracles play a vital role in our lives but don't be obsessed with them. This is another way for the negative power to keep you away from your primary goal in life.

You must keep stressing your goal towards God-realisation and achieving that will be a miracle in the real sense.

# MIND

The mind is the key player in our lives. It dominates all the lower bodies, including the soul body. The mind under control is a good servant; otherwise, it is a bad Master. The soul body is the reality; it is wrapped up in other bodies to present itself on the physical plane. The wrapping sequence is as soul; within the mental, causal and astral and the one representing is physical. This body is used to communicate and shield the soul from coarse vibrations.

The vitality of the physical body is dependent on the other bodies. Any unbalance in the finer bodies will reflect on the physical body becoming unwell. All lower bodies have limitations, as the physical body cannot travel any higher or the other bodies cannot express themselves on this planet. The mind has its branches on all planes. It can travel from the Physical to the mental plane but it cannot go any higher than the subconscious plane, as it is still part of the lower worlds.

It is destroyable and the last body to leave the soul. Once the soul leaves its residence, the first body it picks up is the mental body. The soul has very fine vibrations. It requires some kind of cover or wrapping as clothing for protection. Without this cover, the soul may be here in this world but our eyes will never see it. It is very similar to the wandering souls who lost their lives by accident. We know them as spirits or ghosts.

The physical body is the leader in this world and all the other bodies are in the background. This is why the soul has no say in this world. All bodies, including the soul, have to express themselves through physical bodies. The mind is responsible for creating all sorts of karma. Without the mind, all other bodies would be without direction. It is very similar to a magnet; The magnetic field will run in all directions when it is not fully magnetised.

Without this direction, the experience of the soul will not be complete. The mind helps the soul to experience and all other bodies are designed for this purpose. The worse karma we create, the better the experience will be for the soul. These bad experiences will happen naturally as we go through our lower lives, such as minerals, birds and mammals.

These lower-life experiences will bring the soul to the human level. Upon reaching the human level, we are more or less civilised but the first few lives may be human; our behaviour will be semi-human or more or less animal in status. This is why you will notice that some men or women are humans but their behaviour is abnormal. They will improve and be very intelligent and more civilised than you can imagine in time.

This is why we recommend giving everyone their psychic space. You cannot ask anyone to do something they are not capable of doing. During early incarnations, the soul is silent. It does not have much say in the direction of life. The physical and astral bodies are very active. With time, we become balanced overall and maturity takes place. This process could take up to fifty thousand years; at present, our lifespan is eighty years on average.

All the bodies have a fair amount of experience. The struggle begins between the soul and the mind. The soul wants to leave the lower worlds and the mind is very active and running in all directions. The soul body is nudging the mind and other bodies to create spiritual karma. Before the final departure, the soul has to undo whatever it has done. It is called unfoldment.

It has to open up like a flower to give the fragrance of fine vibrations. Anyone who comes into your presence feels blessed. These are the signs of spiritually awakened souls, better known as saints. These fine vibrations are within but they reflect in your aura. They express through 'Tawega' or known as the Master's gaze. Anyone in the presence of the Master feels better and most of their problems disappear.

The mind is powerful as an obstacle to overcome. You cannot win over the mind; you must follow the golden rule; 'Do not resist evil.' If you do, it will be a never-ending story. We must stay in balance. The mind is the storehouse of desires which spring up like weeds. It is the leading cause of suffering in this world. If we stand still, we can feel thousands of desires. The entity behind all this is the mind.

If something you missed in early life but you loved it so much, you always want to relive it if possible. So, you try to recreate the same scene or situation. All these are desires and they swing through the mind-body into the past, present and future. All our plans for the future are desires. If we live in the present moment, the cravings will be less and our suffering will cease but the mind will not let us sit patiently.

It is the nature of its ability. It is the attachment state of consciousness that drives us to have desires. We must live our life of detachment and contentment through our endeavour of spiritual practice. There is one very deceiving desire that most people are not aware. Upon asking many people, 'What do you want to do in life? we hear a very common answer. 'I would like to help mankind.' This is a very famous line for present leaders, politicians and saints who want to gain popularity.

Helping others is a very negative approach. The idea and intentions are good but it will keep you grounded as another desire in the lower world. This kind of desire looks and sounds good for the emotional side of human nature and attracts everyone. It can make you a leader overnight. The word 'leading' will take you off the track. You can help your fellow humans by all means but neutral or detached. You are supporting and at the same time, you are not helping.

Once you feel others are poor, you feel like helping; it is human nature. But once you know your fellow humans have enough health and wealth, you feel very reluctant to help because you know they do not need it. In the same way, achieve Self and God-realisation for yourself and lead your fellow humans to do the same. Be an example so others feel that you are the person to look up.

Once they are on the move to create good karma, their health and wealth will improve. That way, you have helped them naturally and in return, they helped themselves. God helps those who help themselves. This was a spiritual way of expressing it. This example can be used on the physical level to achieve your goals. We feel sorry for our fellow humans when they are suffering. It is their creation of bad karma responsible for their present conditions.

Nothing is permanent. We have laws that are a replica of the astral plane. Once someone commits a crime, such as murder or theft, the judge passes a sentence, which outlines a period. Once the accused serves time behind bars, the accused is free again. In the same way, once bad karma has been paid off, your misery will be over. This is the physical way of expressing it.

Eventually, all things and situations will fall into place. Kal or negative power, is running the show. Kal is the chief; the mind and other bodies work under its instructions. Kal controls every activity and has many subordinates to fulfil its task. The mind is one of the main instruments which operate on auto-mission and it does the job very well.

Once all the karmas are balanced, the soul has to ask permission from Kal to pass through its gates. Kal or Brahm are very lovely and polite people to deal with. They are only concerned with the soul's spiritual welfare. The mind keeps everybody on their toes, generation after generation. The mind is just an instrument that the Spirit activates; otherwise, it is as dead as anything but it cannot be seen by any physical means.

Once the soul has left the lower worlds forever, the mind, causal and astral bodies will disperse themselves into the atmosphere accordingly on respective planes. On the physical, we follow the procedure of burial or cremation. The Spirit cannot be seen, just as electricity cannot be seen when running through the wires. However, it can express itself through the lightbulb. The Spirit is felt when all the lower bodies are functioning.

Awakened people can feel the presence of the Spirit. There is a lower and higher mind and the spiritual mind. The Spirit use the mind to express itself in the lower worlds. The mind has four modes of quality or faculty in action, which are mentioned in Hinduism and many other spiritual scriptures.

**Chittah**: It receives its impressions through the eyes. This faculty considers form, beauty, colours, rhythm and harmony. What it likes or dislikes and passes its judgement to the intellectual side of the person, which is buddhi.

**Manas**: This faculty receive impressions through the senses of smell, taste, hearing and feeling. What it likes or dislikes and passes its judgement over to buddhi.

**Buddhi**: This is the intellectual side of the mind. It is often expressed as cosmos, consciousness or Buddha consciousness. Fine thoughts are defined by this faculty. It has the power to decide and discriminate what it has received from chittah and manas and pass its findings to the ahankar for final execution.

**Ahankar**: This part of the mind receives the subtotal information of the last three faculties and finally, this is the court of judgement. Being the executioner, it is called the 'I' or 'ego' part of the mind. This part of the mind identifies itself. This makes the person more or less intellectual than the others. This faculty makes you say, 'Therefore, I am.' If this faculty produces good thoughts and actions, it acts as the higher or spiritual mind; otherwise, it is vanity.

The main procedure is from soul to physical. The soul is the messenger to convey its information through the mind and Spirit is the activator of the mind. The Mind has to go through the astral body, which receives the information and then expresses it through the physical body. It is very easy to work if the mind is trained, then all the situations are under control, as the soul wishes.

**Subconscious mind:** Etheric plane. This is the higher type of mind and it is very close to the soul plane. It has excellent vibrations. Often, people mistake it for the soul plane. This is the dividing line between the lower and higher planes. This is where all the subconscious actions come from. It is the region of unknown powers, such as ESP, clairvoyance and other psychic qualities.

Those people close to this state of mind will have many fantasies. When a person is sitting silently, many unknown and extraordinary experiences occur. It is more or less a neutral mind.

# POSSESSION

We want to possess all. Whatever we see, it should be ours. This feeling is not the same as gaining material security. This is the field of attachment or moha. It is based more on human relationships than on material gains. The Individuals going through this dramatic experience are willing to lose all their security for the chance of achieving possession of someone. This is falling in love with someone and it is a very emotional experience to go through.

The person becomes a daydreamer. Their thoughts are occupied most waking hours and even through the dream process. The moth loves to make circles around the light because it enjoys its company. In the same way, this person's thoughts are on one subject only. It does not matter what other tasks are at hand. If both are on the same wavelength, that is well and good and could lead to marriage and living happily ever after. Then the state of possessiveness vanishes and everyday life begins.

If it is a one-sided fatal attraction, it becomes painful for either side. One person is mentally disturbed and becomes the stalker and the other becomes the victim, living in fear. Either way, it is not working out. If there are karmas to be shared, then nothing can stop you. If not, it will be a big struggle, mental torture and a loss of valuable time. We are living in the material world. Nothing is permanent. This is the trap set by the negative force to keep you off the right track.

This is the test and it happens in the life of everyone. Let alone ordinary people, even the saints, get trapped in this. History is full of examples. There are quite a few historical stories in Hinduism. We can divert our attention to experience God. I know it will be a challenging task but it could be rewarding.

There is a story of one couple in the olden days. The husband loved his wife so much he did not want to part from her even for a minute. He followed her everywhere. The wife was very wise and one day, she said, 'If you love God as much you love me, do you know you can have God in your life? It clicked into his mind and he began to meditate as much as possible. Nowadays, he is a very famous historical saint.

It will help if your energy is directed to benefit you and the people around you. No one can possess anyone. God created us all in its image to do its work. 'How can you possess someone else when you do not even possess yourself? Give up all unproductive thoughts. Whatever you do, do it productively and in the name of God. You cannot possess God but become part of its spiritual scheme. Stop all your struggles and let God possess you.

You are found wanted.

# JEALOUSY

Jealousy is the offspring of anger, as many religions agree upon, especially in the eastern world. There are five passions of the mind responsible for bringing the individual's downfall. Most holy men recommend that we learn to balance them individually to lead a balanced and peaceful life. This trait, **jealousy,** has been responsible for much destruction.

It works from the lowest to the lowest and the highest. The word itself dictates who is in charge. From the African jungles to the red Indians, people fought under jealousy about who would be the next chief. If the chief has selected his successor to pass his authority to this person, one or two don't agree. They would do everything to bring him down and give him a bad name to show that he was not worthy of the title.

Due to jealousy, many governments failed and this will carry on for a long time until some spiritual realisation comes. This is the power play and jealousy is the booster factor. Since the middle of the last century, the pace of this world has sped up enormously. It is totally out of control at speed it is going now. Minds are running wild and people have wild imaginations and jealousy is in action.

The jealousy factor is evident in the families between brothers and sisters when they have something you want or think should be yours. You will notice this jealousy factor is not based on anger alone. If something is materially involved, such as money, property or any other gain, it becomes part of the greed. If it consists of a love triangle; it is part of the attachment and there is an extreme passion of jealousy between the lovers.

It does not matter if two men fight over one woman or two women fight for one man. Many murders have been committed under the influence of jealousy. There is always one thing in mind; If I can't have it, no one else can. When one of them ends up in jail, only then do they come to their senses, what has taken place. It is far too late to turn the clock back.

Nowadays, all five passions have become part of this negative trait. A very high percentage of people spend most of their time under this influence and rarely are successful. Most of their creative time is wasted on making negative plans. The plans always involve bringing the other person down to their level. The jealous person will create obstacles wherever possible, using whatever is in their power.

It is very common among people of eastern origin when they cannot do anything themselves; they get the help of black magicians to cast a spell on their opponents. Some spells have time limits, such as three, five or seven years. The spells cannot be reversed unless the victim knows someone to remove them. Otherwise, the victim will suffer in silence and the effect could be lifelong. The jealous person living in this state of consciousness is very dangerous and can create grave situations for others, with disastrous results.

As the jealous person attempts to victimise his opponents, at the same time, he is the victim of these two or three passions himself. The harm you are trying to give someone harms you first. If your effort is successful, the victim will only be harmed; otherwise, you are the victim of yourself. Most of your creative or progressive time is spent under this influence and you are the channel for the Kal power.

If the opponent becomes aware of your attacks and they use similar power to answer back, then physical destruction is inevitable on both sides. Often this leads to murder. In other cases, small fights take place. Once you awake out of this state and realise your mistakes, the word **sorry**, which is often said, is not good enough. The negative karmas you have created remain answerable.

Some people arc blinded by jealousy; the amount of karma they create can take a few lifetimes to clear. Any person who follows the spiritual path must be careful. You are the open channel for the Spirit. You could be taken over by the opposing force very quickly. A serious student of spiritual studies must be careful not to be victimised by this negative trait. This word, jealousy, should not exist in your dictionary and if it does, you are not ready for this kind of teaching.

You probably are better off in your previous religion or spiritual studies. Once you become aware of this negativity, you should work on it. A sincere request made to the Master will help balance this negative trait. The word jealousy has destroyed so many and will destroy you, so be aware of it. This one word, jealousy, could be more dangerous than all the five passions put together and the spiritual success you are looking for will never exist.

The decision is yours.

# DARK NIGHT OF THE SOUL

This is one of the most significant achievements during our spiritual journey. As we follow the Master, everything seems good and situations are pleasant. We feel happy and our experiences on the inner and outer are excellent. After two years of following, you are connected to the light and sound. The working off your karma is accelerated.

There is a huge backlog of karma from many previous lives to be balanced to achieve spiritual freedom as this is your last life on earth. We have to work very hard to make sure to achieve our goal. The soul is always connected to the light and sound but the Master makes it live. This period of two years is to discipline yourself according to our teaching. Living Master focuses on your progress and decides that you are ready to experience live; light and sound.

It shows your progress from the physical to entering into the spiritual side of life. You have worked very hard and the Master is and was watching and helping at every turn to make sure you achieved this. This is the first step. The second step will be to progress from the light and sound to Self-realisation. The third step is God-realisation. Since you are connected to the light and sound, the Master guides you in the inner and outer to build up the stamina to take the next step.

The next step is slightly harder and there is no time limit to succeed. You will be tested many times and will fail many times. The Master makes sure you go through each test and pass with flying colours. When Master knows that you are ready for the next step, he leaves you alone. The question arises within, 'What will I do? When you are left alone, he withdraws any previous support you depended on. He pretends that way but he is always watching.

He does this to make sure you are using your own effort to pass the test. This test is crucial to know that you can survive on your own later in life. When you become the Master of your universe. This is a crucial period for the follower; you have depended on the Master's guidance in the past, at this point, the helping facility is withdrawn. It becomes the dark night of the soul for the follower.

When followers feel that they are standing alone, all their hopes go berserk. They feel let down and isolated. The Master gives no hint to the follower that he will do that. After this situation, which Master has purposefully created, the Seekers do not even realise what they are going through. Seeker is suffering physical and mental torture every day and is puzzled. The Seeker doesn't know what to do. The seeker does not feel the presence of the Master.

The spiritual exercises will be a mental hash-bash. You do not feel like doing them. You don't even want to pick up the spiritual books, let alone read them. You don't even feel like communicating with other followers. You almost want to give up the teachings, if that is possible but something within keeps you going. Any prayer or petitions to the Master do not seem to work; no answers are given.

The Master does all this purposely. He is trying to stretch you to the maximum, like a rubber band, one more pull and it will snap. This can carry on from a month to a few years. You will feel as if you are in the wilderness. One day, you will get a nudge from somewhere, maybe a paragraph from a book or someone you meet who is positive. He puts some words of wisdom in your ear; this will give you a new lease on life.

This will be your realisation point to know what you are going through. Once you realise, you will bounce back to pull yourself together. Now you love to do all the things you did not want to touch before. Once you realise that you are going through the dark night of the soul, it does not take long to come out of it. The strange thing is when you are going through the dark night of the soul; the Master will not let you feel what you are going through.

You begin to draw your conclusions and walk onto the road of suffering. During this process, much of your karmas are balanced and a strong foundation is being built for the future; nothing can easily shake you. This experience occurs after the light and sound initiation and before the soul initiation. These tests are based on the physical-psychic and mental levels. All the saints have to go through this psychic barrier. If you can't make it through, then you are the struggler.

If you break this barrier and succeed in crossing all the boundaries, then you will be unstoppable to proceed into the world of being. Now you can say, 'Yes, I have done it!' Some make it through relatively easy, while others find it difficult. Never feel discouraged; one day, all the followers will make it and guide the new ones in what to do. Your courage will set all the examples. Now you are not stuck in the dark night of the soul. You are the way-shower, the traveller and the Master of your universe.

# DEPRESSION

There are quite a few different types of Depression. 'What is depression? When a person feels low in spirits, physically and mentally, daily. The leading cause of depression is our multitude of problems. These problems include domestic, financial, work and health issues, losing a loved one, bullying at school or outside, etc. They all lead the individual to feel very low. You have a mental breakdown when you cannot take any more pressure from the situation.

It depends on how severe the attack is. Sometimes it can lead to suicide. Most people who commit suicide suffer from depression; otherwise, it is not easy to take one's own life. Anyone at any age can suffer from depression. Some are suffering from minor attacks, while others have severe attacks. In life, everyone goes through this experience at least once. Often, we are depressed but we don't realise it until someone points it out to us and tells us to be careful.

Sometimes we only realise it when we become hospitalised. Sometimes, the depression appears unrelated to any problem and disappears with time. Time is a great healer. Women have a higher incidence of depression than men; they suffer more from depression and migraines. The percentage of young children (under the age of ten years) is low, as their minds are fresh and they do not suffer as quickly. The incidence among teenagers is slightly higher as they grow out of childhood and their hormones change.

Their behaviour pattern changes and study problems begin to arise. As some grow faster than others, they start bullying the other children, who are weak and lonely. This leads to worse depression and even more severe consequences in some children. Men and women both have many avenues to catch this deadly sickness. Marriage problems and if not married, loneliness is not healthy. Personalities change with age and social status, loss of property or fear of losing something very near and dear to us.

The diagnosis must be left to the professionals in this field. These people have gone through proper training, which teaches them about medicine and human behaviour. Their diagnosis will decide the type of depression a person is suffering from. The symptoms they are looking for include the following.

Irritable mood or behaviour which was not there before.
Loss of interest in life (feeling of uselessness).
Inability to enjoy jokes (love of misery).
Failure to sleep (failure to calm down).
Tiredness and energy loss (could also be due to diabetic conditions).
Weight loss (could be related to other symptoms).
Thoughts of death or suicidal plans.
Loss of concentration (blankness of mind).
At least half the above symptoms indicate that they are suffering from depression. There are a few types.

**Postnatal depression**: This usually happens after the birth of a woman's firstborn. This is due to rapid hormonal changes and it leads to irritable behaviour, being easily tearful and difficulty playing with the newborn. It is an emotional experience and turns into depression. Failure to get proper sympathetic support from the partner or family can also lead to depression.

**Manic depression**: This type of depression involves mood swings, high or low. Sometimes they can be normal, as though nothing happened and at other times, they can exhibit anxious behaviour. Actions include dirty (abusive) language, loss of memory, repetition of words, refusal to take medicine, fear of others and unhealthy body/facial changes.

**Seasonal affective disorder**: This type of depression happens at certain times, generally in autumn or early winter. When daylight changes, our life pattern also changes due to weather changes. This kind of sadness may happen every year at the same time.

**Hallucinations**: This is a widespread type of depression. If a person receives information and cannot handle it, this could be the cause but there could be other reasons. You hear sounds in your head and see visions, like ghostly figures. You see and listen to them, although they are not real. Sometimes people take this depression as a psychic attack. Seeing ghosts is another phase of depression.

There is a tendency to get involved in arguments or fights without knowing the consequences or being easily irritable. Otherwise, you are a calm person.

**Dementia**: This is a decline in mental ability due to a damaged brain or brain cells. It can lead to loss of memory, concentration and perception. Sufferers might feel confused or exhibit restlessness, repetitive behaviour, irritability, tearfulness or disturbed sleep.

**Antisocial depression:** People suffering from this depression have no tolerance. Short tempers lead to violence in public. Sufferers exhibit an I don't care attitude in public. They do not feel part of society and cannot maintain long-term relationships.

**Bulimia:** This kind of depression is a fairly common one. It is an eating disorder marked by overeating and making yourself sick by vomiting food, punishing yourself or avoiding calories. This can lead to poor health and dramatic weight loss.

**Anxiety:** This is a feeling of uneasiness when things are not going your way. Upon experiencing dissatisfaction, the person could have physical symptoms, such as sweating, high pulse rate and quick breathing. Some even suffer a fever. It could become a lifelong habit. Positive thinking, relaxing your mind, deep breathing and taking little breaks help.

Other types of depression related to mental disorders affect the sufferer and society. Depression should be avoided because it is not a good experience to go through. Self-help remedies can be followed. An intelligent person is as good as a doctor because you are the first to know that you are suffering from something and take immediate precautions to avoid further damage. Your doctor will only come to know when things go out of hand.

Many depressed people use alcohol to forget their problems. There is nothing that cannot be sorted out. To any question, there is always an answer. As a result, people become alcoholics and ruin their health, both mentally and physically, with organ failure and in many cases, they are hospitalised. Never lose hope. Take control of your life positively and be in the driving seat. Now you are the Master of your destiny. No one likes to be around a depressed person, so do not become one.

**Self-help remedies**: You should make some effort to help yourself. Or someone else could make an effort to help you come out of this illness. It helps when someone talks positively and provides much-needed moral support with a happier mood.

**Social activities**: If you socialise, your loneliness will disappear. Join sports clubs, which are suitable for exercising. It is essential for the vitality of the body and mind and increases sociability. Good health helps to ward off depression. Create new hobbies. It will entertain your mind, which is responsible for loneliness.

**Charity events**: Join charity events to help socialise and make new friends.

**Diet**: Control of diet is significant. Some foods have adverse effects on our bodies, making us feel irritable. In addition, overweight people are at high risk for depression, so diet control is necessary.

**Movies**: Avoid depressing films and watch funny movies that provide a good laugh. Laughter is good for health. Avoid any sad situations and find something that helps raise your vibrations. Laugh at yourself, if possible.

Good health to you.

# CURSE

It took me some time to understand why Master controls power flow through his Seekers. If they have full authority, they could be very destructive to others. Most of the time, we get frustrated, being the innocent party. People take every advantage and are ready to do their worst. Most of the time, the people who attack you, are jealous and resentful of failure.

When they cannot achieve what you have, they will find some cheap way to bring you down to their level. It could be a physical attack or an official report or if nothing else works, they may even resort to black magic. In the olden days, the saints used to have full spiritual powers. Most of them were the Masters of the hostile forces; it is why they were temperamental most of the time. So, if anyone irritated them even a little bit, they cursed their victims immediately.

The curse used to work instantly. If the saints used the words, you turn into stone. The victim would indeed be turned into stone, a statue, blinded, crippled and cursed with death. Instead of undergoing spiritual unfoldment, they were more interested in cursing people. It was like an act of quick revenge. The damage was done to the people and themselves to create heavy karmas that had to be balanced over a few lifetimes.

A moderate approach is better. If we keep calm, the situations will die down as soon as they spring up. The best policy is to keep your calm and patient and things will fall into place. As the saying goes, 'You reap what you sow.' Whoever tries to harm you will pay, one way or the other.

This is the law of karma.

# HEAVEN OR HELL?

Heaven or hell is one of the most misinterpreted subjects from its early days until today. The pictures have been drawn to create fear factors within the masses to control them and it does work to a certain extent. The fear within makes them think twice before they commit any wrongdoings. This message by the early saints works for the good of the whole.

For example; a person is put into a pot of boiling oil or thrown alive into the fire. You are hanging upside down for years or some horrible beast is tearing your body apart. Jailed indefinitely or thrown into a well full of snakes. You cannot get out until you have served your time, which was allotted against your misdeeds. Any negative picture you can think of is in the book of code and conduct of religions.

If this helps keep you on the right track, I think it is a brilliant idea! All religious writings aim to keep you close to God and away from the Kal's wonderland. But once in a while, everyone wants to glimpse the wonderland, as it attracts the mind. Adam and Eve ate the fruit of the tree of knowledge and the wheel of karma rolled forever.

The world is this 'fruit'; it surrounds us, enticing us at every corner. Most religions have their commandments or codes of conduct. All have the same message; do not eat this fruit any further. Whatever has been consumed so far, try to digest it and pay its price accordingly. Once the price is paid, you are free to leave. Codes and conducts show the ways to pay. I am sure you will find something to your taste.

The pictures of heaven are drawn delightfully. You are sitting under a tree in a beautiful garden, a few angels are taking care of you and you are having the time of your life. Some of the pictures you have never seen before. For example, you are at a lovely holiday resort. Other images could depict you on a seat next to the lord of karma to help him in his decisions. You will be eating the best food ever or sitting in a state of bliss and peaceful surroundings.

You can draw thousands of pictures in your imagination. If these pictures help you to lead a good life and be a good person, who hardly conducts a bad deed, then I think this is the beginning for you to go beyond. As long as you are below the soul plane, you are still living on the terms of Kal, otherwise known as hell. All your experiences are negative or positive in the lower world. You are still in the trap and liable to the system of reincarnation.

These religions, which stress these two points very strongly (heaven or hell), operate from the mental level only. They have no further insight beyond these lower worlds. Their Masters never went further than the mental plane and taught what they knew. Religion begins where science ends and pure spiritual experience begins where religion ends. This is the sequence; science, religion and pure Spirit. But in the future, the arrangement will be religion, science and pure Spirit.

All these pictures or images represented by the past Masters are incorrect. The King of the Dead is responsible for counting your good and bad deeds and balancing them out.

He decides accordingly and prepares your next incarnation on Earth. You are allowed once more to balance your karma in the best way possible. Contrary to most religious belief; The Lord of Karma does not clear your karma in his place.

If you are punished in his place for misdeeds, that means you have become karma-less and your motivation to come into the physical finishes. Therefore, further experience for the soul will be halted. The whole purpose of the soul's journey will be lost. Upon judgement, you are sent downwards into the physical plane to carry on working off your karma. God has created all souls to be equal, 'Where do we differ from each other? This is what we call karma.

Accordingly, you may be born as a beggar, prince, born blind or without limbs. All these states are part of your karma. It is based on your previous earnings. It is the decision of the Lord of Karma and sometimes, the soul decides to work off its karma this way, on the physical.

**Heaven or hell:** Both are part of the same coin, as we say, 'head or tail.' They are both subject to positive or negative; day and night, man and woman, good and bad, ugly and beautiful. These terms are not in balance; they are extremes on either side. As long as we are subject to opposites, we are still in hell. It does not matter which plane you are on.

Once you have balanced yourself out of this duality, you will enter the pure spiritual worlds. After experiencing heaven and hell, the lower worlds are like a toy for a child. As they grow up, these toys are meaningless to them. You focus on present needs and seek further. The true heaven is in the pure spiritual worlds, where all the situations are in the state of being.

There are no opposites of any kind. It is beyond the conditions of matter, energy, space or time. You can return to the lower worlds with your own free will to assist in the cause of God, as most of the saints do. Once you have crossed the dividing line into the lower worlds again, you become liable to create karma. Good or bad, the choice is yours.

# POWER

God is omnipotent; therefore, God's world is run by power. The world of being on neutral power. The lower worlds use negative and positive power. This world is a mix of spiritual, psychic, material and political power. Political power is used to control the masses. A few countries are known to be the superpower countries, such as USA and USSR to dominate other nations. There is a psychic power to control people and families. Only a few are aware of spiritual power. All these powers are tough to control.

The power is given to someone who cannot control it could be dangerous and destructive. The recipient of power must have the stamina to withstand its strength; otherwise, it will tear him down and the person becomes out of balance and worse can be expected in that state. When passing over the power on the spiritual path, the leader must test the individual's capabilities. In the last century, we have experienced catastrophic results because the power has fallen into the wrong hands.

This has caused much destruction to their respective countries and caused a loss of control over other nations. All wars are fought to gain power. History keeps repeating itself and it will do so in the future. Power must be given wisely and used wisely. The wise person will use control correctly or ignore it if possible. Political powers control most religious places. Elections are fought on a large scale to gain control of these spiritual places.

I hope they understand the meaning of these places. We go there to pray to the almighty God. If we cannot find peace in such places, 'Where should we go? This will lead future generations to seek peace somewhere else. Spiritual education is the basic foundation for the soul to pursue further and attain its final destination. If possible, in this lifetime. All religions are very near and dear to my heart, as they provide the basic knowledge to prepare the Seeker.

Ancient saints are known to walk away from their religion to achieve their spiritual goals. Most saints were condemned by their religious circle because the religious body did not like them to walk away from their sect or system. These souls were brave and adventuresome. They challenged the system of their respective religions. These great souls are known as Guru Nanak, Kabir and Buddha, to name just a few. This is not the end; it will carry on in the future until the end of this world.

Now we are going to discuss spiritual power. God chooses one particular person at a time to represent itself in this world. This person is always in the male form. The female cannot take this responsibility for many physical reasons. Many other saints claim to run this world. Maybe the saint himself is not claiming but his followers believe it.

The basic information about this person is that he is not an ordinary man. He is born a saint by birth and has been on this earth many times before. This time, he has been chosen for a special mission to become the living Master of the time, who will be the only one responsible to God. This person was karma-less in the spiritual world before his present journey into the physical.

As his planned birth occurs, he becomes subject to physical laws but he is a law unto himself and can supersede the physical laws to the required situations but he seldom does that. He is given special protection from birth so he does not lose himself in this wonderland and stray from his allotted mission to spread the message of God.

His mission is to return the souls ready to leave this world to achieve spiritual freedom, as they are almost karma-less in the lower planes. This person is made aware of his mission in this life at a very early age. Due to his personal spiritual experiences, he knows that he is not part of the crowd and people nearby also note strange happenings to find him extraordinary. As a particular person in the family, he is respected and he is the target of jealousy because he gets more attention and respect.

A few will not tolerate him and give him a hard time to the fullest extent. This chosen one is not supposed to reveal his true identity. Instead, he may choose to suffer in silence. God has given him enough strength to face the whole world alone. These family torments are like a toy to him and he laughs silently too. As Jesus said, 'Father, forgive them, for they know not what they do,' but these people will be held responsible for their misdeeds and will pay accordingly.

Sometimes this chosen one also feels down just like anyone else, as he is subject to karma, pain, pleasure, happiness and suffering. Sometimes in despair, he raises his hands, pointing at God, 'Why have you forsaken me? He lives and acts just like anyone else but secretly, he lives according to his future mission. Like any prince, he knows he will be the future king, so he cannot act or behave like the crowd.

From childhood until his mission, he spends his time with friends and in school to educate himself on a worldly level. But during this process, he has never forgotten who he is and what his future assignments are. Although he has spiritual knowledge from past lives, he has to be trained again in this life. He is already an awakened soul on the spiritual level. He always has his guardian angels from birth.

There is another circle of Masters, who are the special chosen ones by God. They maintain all the universes and watch closely to ensure he gets all the required training. They visit to show their presence and to check on his spiritual progress. The chosen person is introduced to all the lords for any required training. He is given access to all the spiritual temples to study. The purification of his spiritual body is explained in the chapter '**Anami-Lok.**'

Now he is ready to take over as the new living Master as soon as the present Master is ready to retire. On the day of exchanging this spiritual mantle, it is done in the presence of known spiritual Masters. He receives infinite powers. In physical, he is limited but spiritually, he is everywhere. He can handle this power, as he has been trained to withstand the strength. Nothing can go to his head unless this power is given to the wrong person by mistake.

This seldom happens but if it does, the power can go to his head and bring lots of unknown destruction to the self and others. Do not misuse this power, even on a minor scale; it will backfire on you one day. Those who turn against their own Master, I don't know how they can withstand this guilt for the rest of their life. The true Master will carry on his mission whether he is known or not. It does not bother him one bit.

On the spiritual level, no one loses anything but he will be out of touch with everyone on the physical level, which will be a loss to many. He listens only to the dictates of God and fulfils his mission according to his allotted time. He prepares the next person to take over when he retires. His future assignment could be here in the physical or in the spiritual worlds.

The Spirit will carry on forever. To some, it is power.

# PRINCE OR PAUPER

This subject is very close to my heart. We need to find out who we are. It is one of the most remarkable discoveries for some, especially those unaware of who they are. I knew myself from a very early age and my mission in life. My quest began at a very early age to be close to my creator, the real king. I could not help thinking differently from others of my generation.

Many of my friends never knew what I was thinking in school, college or in private life. I was dealing with them every day, just like any other boy in the neighbourhood. This was my private world. I always knew I belonged to God and God belonged to me. By birth, we are all princes of God. God is the creator; it created its world and universes, from the physical to the Ocean of Love and Mercy and beyond.

This is the kingdom of God. God created this for us to experience; otherwise, God was alone and these universes would have been empty or void spaces. This void is filled by its presence or Spirit. There is no such place, space or void where it does not exist. If we cannot feel its existence, this is due to our physical limitations. If we go beyond our physical senses, we will know all.

Jesus Christ had this awareness. This is why he is called the 'Son of God.' We are all sons or daughters of God; it is a physical expression. Jesus Christ mentioned the Father many times and in many places. God is the king; we are princes of God and should act like princes. 'Have we forgotten who we are? Nowadays, we are acting like beggars. We beg for everything when rightfully everything is ours. We only have to know and have it.

There is a theory of assumption. We assume something; it will happen so that you can have it. You should believe everything is yours anyway. I am not suggesting grabbing whatever comes your way. Whatever is there, let it be and enjoy it. We have lost awareness of our true identity; we have become or are acting like beggars. We beg through our prayers, always asking for something in return.

People go to temples to pray and donate a few coins. There is always something in the back of their mind, such as asking for financial improvement. This is the first demand of most people; a good job, good health, and good children. The list is endless. We have become so negative; we want everything for free. If possible, we would have grabbed God for free; we cannot do it because the curtain is drawn over our senses.

My suggestion is; Go for it and it is free. Very few people ask for the good of the whole. Even if they do, they don't mean it. You will receive what is yours and no one can take it away from you. It will not come as hard as you try if something is not supposed to come your way. It will never come unless you let go of it. Please leave it to the Spirit to work on.

Principally, 'See the word, if reduced, it is a prince.' We are supposed to give and this is the main attribute that God has invested within us and not to receive. The more we give, the more we receive. This is like a bank balance. If we do not invest in our account, it will be closed unless we apply for a loan. The loan is very similar to receiving something which is not ours in the first place and we are in debt (karma), so we have to pay it back sooner or later.

Therefore, we should be on the giving side, not the receiving end. It is the belief of people throughout this world that God is here to give. To feel the presence of God, they have created temples, churches and many other holy places. Millions of people attend these places to show love to God; because God has already given us that. It is only getting back what already has been given to us.

I hope you will catch the principle. Learn to give and it will return to you manyfold. I don't believe in prayers, as most religions do. I hardly prayed because I did not feel the need for it. Sometimes I pray for other people when they cannot ask or don't know how to ask. I feel that God is the king and we are all its heirs. God is the Father and we are all its children. We take the example of a mother and her tiny baby.

This is how I behave with God and it is successful. A tiny baby always gets its needs when hungry. The mother always knows what the requirements are and at what time. The baby does not ask; the parents always know when and what to provide to fulfil that child's needs. In the same way, God knows precisely; what we need and when we need it. By asking through petitions and prayers, we tell God what to do.

As I said before, 'God knows when and what to give.' We only feel frustrated when we ask for something before it is time. Be near to God and find your way of doing it. Build up that relationship. The stronger the relationship, the less you need to ask; otherwise, you will feel like an unwanted child who feels insecure at every step of life. You lose confidence in life and live in the hope that something will come your way.

Be positive and build up this relationship and you will be surprised that things will come your way without even asking.

I am trying to make the point here to make the relationship of high and all these things will come to you. We are asking for small meaningless things. In the same way, God has numerous attributes and people try to adopt a few or one at a time. God is like a tree. 'Why should we go for its branches when we can have all of it? If we go for the whole tree, everything will be added to you.

We are the princes, not the paupers, so start acting like princes and be counted as one of its' own.

# LET IT GO

We have so many situations in our lives and they bother us so much. Sometimes you feel mentally torn apart. Problems arise and sometimes, they are created by others. As a result, you are hurt and feel low. The more you hang on to the problems, the more they will bother you. There is nothing to be gained out of this other than mental torture. Let go of it as soon as possible and feel free.

It is the same as when you have lost a loved one. The attachment bothers you so much and it is not very easy to let go of it. Let them go mentally. Set them free. That way, spiritually, they will be happy and in return, you will be satisfied too. Sometimes the Master also creates the situation as a test. It will drag you down and bother you at every turn and you will be so fed up with it. You feel like a soldier who has just returned home from a lost war.

You give up and say, 'Who cares? I do not wish to write down what I have been through but this is how to do it. As soon as you have done that, you will feel free and notice the situation has resolved itself. The Master's task is complete.

Now you have learned how to let go of it. But the hard way.

# DESTINY

We are here to fulfil our destinies. Either great or small, it depends on our karma. Karma will lead you in the direction of your destiny to be fulfilled. We are born in the right place and at the right time to meet all the conditions. Most people will come and go without a trace. Nobody knows who they are or were because they have not created enough good karma whereby Spirit will bring them into the limelight for the world to see. However, in time, their turn will come.

You will notice that most famous historical figures were very shy and never wanted to step onto the stage. They preferred to shy away and carry on giving their message in silence. When the right time came, they could not hide anymore. The time factor of their life created a situation and the next day, everyone knew them.

> 'What is destiny? You were born to do something extraordinary.

Now, there are two conditions for this. First, it does not matter how hard you try. If you are not to become famous, it will not happen. Secondly, if you are to become famous, you can hide as much as you like but you will be dragged out of your hiding place and into the limelight. God especially sends some gifted people to change the course of history. They will be born into a random family and one day, they will leave that family and get on with their mission and execute it correctly according to the spiritual instructions.

Some are born in a family, where parents are already fulfilling their great destiny but the work has to be carried on as the mission is incomplete. Sometimes this can carry on for a few generations until the task is complete. Their destiny must not be altered in any way. Any alteration can bring great upheaval and many people will be affected. This unexpected change in the lives of those whose course of life has been altered, their life will become like a whirlpool.

This whirlpool will create a catastrophic situation; people are doing what is not supposed to be done, either good or bad. Unexpected situations usually create negative conditions; most people suffer and only a few benefit. There will be some who are unshakeable. It does not matter what happens around them; no one can change their mind or the course of their mission. This change of destiny happens on an immense scale. Only spiritual people are capable of doing this.

It has been done in many religions in the past and it may happen again. We are talking about the people who were destined to be famous but have given their place to somebody else; who is not eligible. Sometimes the people in the family can create conditions where the wrong person is chosen. The people who created the un-destined situation are responsible for the total karmic load of the people who have been affected as their lives are altered.

'What happens to the destined person whose life has been side-tracked? 'What will they be doing in this situation as their lives are wasted? They were supposed to be doing whatever they came for or sent here. I am sure sometimes they feel angry because they are in a situation where they are not supposed to be. They may feel as if they are trapped, forced to spend the rest of their lives, similar in a vegetative state. They are superior souls and take it as 'The Will of God' and silently move on with their lives.

Silence and spiritual stamina are their strength when people around them never know who they are. They are never angry with God but patiently wait for the next assignment. Now we see two or three examples where destined people were replaced by others who were also great souls but not supposed to be in the limelight. A great example happened a few thousand years ago in Hinduism. This is the story of Sri Ram and Sita.

The great Ramayana is based on this part of history. Sri Ram was a prince who was destined to be the future king. His father, King Dashrath, had three wives and four sons. One of the wives helped the king during the war, so he granted her several wishes. Later, she asked for these wishes to be granted. Sri Ram was to be sent into exile for many years and her son, named Bharat, was to be made king. The king could not refuse, so he granted her promised wishes.

Sri Ram and Sita (wife) and his brother Lakshman went into the jungle and the three of them spent their lives as ordinary people. As the course of destiny was changed, Sita was abducted by King Ravana of Sri Lanka. Wars were fought over this and uncountable people died, especially the men. Imagine the suffering of the children and wives of the dead soldiers and a whole load of karma. Now imagine who was responsible for this.

This is what happens when the course of destiny is changed. Often, the Lord of Karma pre-planned history and situations are bound to happen that way. This is why it is recommended not to enter anyone's psychic space without their permission. This could alter much and the result could be disastrous. We will look at some great people who walked on this earth and fulfilled their destinies.

Guru Nanak was supposed to do business as planned by his father but he was aware of his spiritual mission. As he progressed in life, people learned that he was not an ordinary person. He went against the odds, which were Hinduism and Islam of that day and carried on to spread the message of God, which was 'God is one.' Later, another nine gurus followed him and now the religion is called Sikhism.

Jesus Christ had a similar destiny. St. John of the cross and others knew before his birth. Once born, people would know the Messiah had come. He wasn't interested in doing any regular work. He knew his mission in life. He also went into the wilderness. He was ready for his mission to spread the word of God. He gave us many outstanding examples to follow. By going up on the cross and giving up his life, he became alive in the hearts of his followers.

Moses was another great man as he went in front of the burning bush, where the Lord appeared, gave him the Ten Commandments and told him what his mission was in life.

Mahatma Buddha was born as a prince to lead his nation as the future king. He was a spiritually awakened soul and knew that he was in the wrong place. Despite all the palaces his father had built for him to enjoy, he felt uncomfortable. Although he was married and had a son, he still walked off to achieve his spiritual goal. After many hardships, he received the enlightenment and spiritual mission in his life and carried on to preach what he knew.

He was the most peaceful person on Earth. Now he is known worldwide. If he had remained as prince and later become king, I don't think he could have been more famous than now. He knew he had a spiritual destiny to fulfil.

# ASTROLOGY

## Past – Present – Future

Past, present and future are our dream world, our whole life circles around these three gems. These three are the spices of life. The past is our experience and the present motivates for to do something. The future is our wonderland. Most people do not begin their day without knowing their horoscope. Sixty percent of the population views the zodiac star signs every day.

We read our star signs daily in newspapers; nowadays, computers are doing a similar job. If we feed in information, such as name, date and place of birth, it will give us the reading for the whole year. In this chapter, the information will be fundamental. It is all provided to satisfy our minds. The star signs sound optimistic; otherwise, the day will be just another ordinary day.

There are twelve zodiac signs in a year and millions are reading them daily. The ratio is one million people to a star sign in a small country. It could be a few million to a star sign in larger countries. Someone is sitting in an office and writing them every day. Can you imagine; 'How can he dictate the future of millions of people? It is not possible. People are naive enough to believe this is their destiny for the day.

That same writer never misses the opportunity to add a spicy line that attracts everyone. 'If you want to know about your love life, please ring this number.' The mind needs satisfaction. No one can change your destiny. Both good and bad patches in your life are your creation. For some, everyday situations are working fine, while most people face hardships and look for a way to find happiness.

There are many ways to seek past, present and future information but the past is responsible for current conditions. Many professionals can help.

**Janam-patri (horoscope):** It is very famous in India. Hindu saints conquered this phenomenon in the olden days, which fascinates our minds. At a similar time, it had links to Persia. To have successful reading for the past, present and the future, the birth details such as; date, time and place of birth must be correct.

I will illustrate a story to demonstrate the importance of time. A king and queen were expecting a new arrival in the family. The king made sure that he would note the correct time at the birth of a newborn, down to the seconds. He gave a rubber ball to the midwife and instructed that she rolled the ball out of the delivery room when the child was born. He would catch the ball and note the time.

The king invited a Hindu priest to forecast the child's future based on time and given date. The Janam-patri (Horoscope) was prepared. The prince's future was bright and the king was made aware of his achievements. As time went by, the prince assumed his duties in the kingdom. He achieved more than what his Janam-patri forecasted. The king suspected that Janam-patri was wrong. The Hindu priest was called back to re-check the contents of the Horoscope.

The priest re-checked and found nothing wrong. The pundit was also surprised because the prince achieved more than his predicted forecast. The pundit advised the king to consult a wiser senior pundit and get his opinion. They managed to find one. He looked into the contents of the Horoscope and announced that it was wrong. He asked; what procedure was followed to note the time of birth. He analysed the story and declared that the recorded time was wrong.

'You have noted the time of catching the ball but you forgot to add the additional seconds it took for the ball to roll outside. Now, if you add these extra seconds and re-calculate, you will see what his actual achievements will be.' This is how important it is to have the exact time of birth. Otherwise, you have a Horoscope but it is not yours.

**Tarot cards** are popular in the Western world but the results are not very impressive. When a person is in trouble, they are willing to go anywhere to find some peace in life. I wish some cards could help but it is not that easy. I watched a tarot card reader on TV and he communicated via the telephone. The reader laid the cards on the table and asked the caller to say 'stop' on three cards.

When the caller said 'stop,' the reader had laid three extra cards because there was a time delay in the communication system. In other words, the reader has picked three different cards than what the caller wanted. The reader stated the future according to the cards in his hands. 'What would you expect from these sorts of readings?

**Face-reading**: This procedure has worked over the centuries. Some go by total facial features concerning each other; long face, round face. Some readers go by the countenance on your forehead, which acts as an aura reading to them.

They can feel the state of bliss on your face or vice versa. There are many other theories on face reading. This technique is not bad for providing temporary mental satisfaction.

**Palmistry:** Is famous worldwide. The readings are based on the natural lines in your palm. The experts can relate these lines with your horoscope; palm reading and horoscope go hand in hand. The change in lines of your hand dictates the future. This can be true to a certain degree on a physical level. Your future can be interfered with by psychic attacks. It seems everyone has gone through or will go through this process. The pundits who perform these readings are very famous in India.

The Gypsies are well-known in Europe. Not all lines on your palm determine your fate. Some lines are natural fate lines. Some are formed over the years as your hands carry out manual work. A person holding a pen all day in an office will have different lines than the person holding a hammer. We go through all these avenues of life because we feel insecure or face many unknown hardships. To know the unknown, we have to go beyond physical.

**Astral readings:** Now, we are dealing with the emotional body. Astral readings go beyond all previously discussed readings. The reader must be a psychic expert or a spiritual traveller. Who can rise above the physical to scan the astral body to provide any other information you seek. If, however, you are not satisfied or the problem persists, it may be in the causal body.

**Causal readings:** This body is the storehouse for all our past lives on the physical plane. The reader with this ability can scan all three bodies simultaneously. You don't need to have committed any bad karma for the present condition to exist. These psychic bodies can also get out of balance at some point in life due to psychic attacks. I call them new arrivals. People in the spiritual field can balance psychic bodies to bring peace of mind.

**Mental body:** The experts can spot the unbalanced in aura readings. This is called aura adjustment. Each body carries different shades of colour. Sometimes, these psychic bodies hang outside the physical due to some psychic attack or sudden shock, etc. The person is helpless. The expert is needed at hand.

**Mind-reading:** Mind reading is a very shallow act. It is more or less show business to say, 'I know what is in your mind.' You already know this anyway but it makes you wonder, 'How does he know? Scanning the mental body or adjusting auras is entirely another aspect.

**Subconscious readings:** If the root of the problem is not found anywhere, you have come to the right place. There is an enormous amount of information in the subconscious, gathered over centuries. The imprint on this body can disturb the individual for many lives. Most of these past experiences are related to the fear factor. Family arguments or parents going through a bad patch can reflect on your life. Learn to rise above these negative experiences before leading an everyday life.

**Soul Reading:** Atmic-Vidya; Is beyond the lower bodies or karma. The soul's journey can be traced to its original entry into the lower worlds. The reader typically mentions the lives that he feels are outstanding. A soul reading is the ultimate reading for the soul or the chosen ones. Strong willpower can eliminate any problem; it provides the power to face the situation positively. Most problems are time-related; they come in time and disappear. Never discourage yourself. Spirit is always protecting you.

Create positive karma to experience a bright future.

# LOVE ALL LIFE

We must love all forms of life; it doesn't matter what they are. If we do not, we have not understood the message of our spiritual Master and his teachings. All religions convey a similar statement; God is one; it created us and is within. Any spiritually awakened person comes to the point of realisation that we are souls and as souls, we are minor gods. Being little gods, we are one.

Then who can say; 'I have not seen God? It expresses itself through all forms of life. The soul itself is beyond relations; mother, father, brother, sister, cousins and friends. These are given tags to identify each other physically. This is why we have become more physical and forgotten ourselves as souls. The veil over senses; apart from a few relations, the rest of the world seems like nothing or enemies.

We do not tolerate others if they have more than us. We become jealous and try to steal, either by force or politics; our aim is the same. We must be aware that the other soul is part of us. 'So, what; if that soul has more? It is all ours. If the other soul also has the same awareness, it will never hesitate to give whatever it possesses to others. The decision is made in a split second. Upon asking of the first soul, the second soul will say, 'You want this so that you will have it.' This internal feeling is bliss.

We are all created for a purpose; as many believe, nothing is created as nothing. This is why we take everything for granted. Any weak person is treated as nothing and abused to the fullest extent. This happens in families, at school or at work and on a bigger scale, between countries. Not everyone is as weak as they seem. Sometimes it is an expression of humbleness. We take them for granted without realising their soul is likely more awakened than ours.

We emphasize too much on ourselves or possessions and live in fear of losing what we have. We have created the walls and live in fear so that no one can steal from us. We are protecting something worth nothing and losing awareness as souls, which is beyond price. All countries have created borders and soldiers protect both sides. One side always tries to go over to the other to occupy what they have.

Throughout history, all the great wars have been fought over this. The superpower country always tries to dominate and gain overall control. Under these circumstances, 'What do they know about the soul? Their greed and power drive them beyond their rights and they cross all boundaries to kill whatever gets in their way. Alexander the Great was not satisfied with what he had. Nor was Napoleon and later Hitler of Germany.

They all wanted the whole world in their pocket. But they managed to lose everything they had, even their lives, in the end. It is bizarre; During the wars, all soldiers pray to their God to grant victory over the other side but in fact, both armies are praying to the same God, which is only one. In an army, many soldiers are very religious. It makes me wonder, 'What have they learned from their religion?

They only recite the verses of their religion because they were told to do so. 'Will they ever have time to open up to the teachings? 'Will they discover the truth? We must realise that God is one; we are praying to the same one for our victory. 'Which side do you think God will be on? Neither. You might think God will take the side that commits more rights than wrongs but there is no right or wrong in the world of God.

This is the world of illusion and we are trapped in it. This is why we are claiming our rights. 'Would you harm others if you realised that you are a soul and the other person is a soul too? 'Could you afford to terminate that life? All souls are trying to become assistants to God.

Learn to appreciate the beauty of its creation. The experience will be abundant and you will not be far away from its presence. All the animal kingdom, the one we most likely take advantage of, is part of its creation. If you look into the eyes of any animal, you will feel that it is unique and admire its presence, especially baby animals. How cute and gentle they are. You feel the same love for them as you would your children.

We are mentally superior and we control them. Without this creation, you would not have milk for a cup of tea early in the morning. I feel a bit uncomfortable using the word 'animal' for their description. I am not pointing the finger at non-vegetarians but pause for a minute and wonder at the beauty of its creation.

The sea is responsible for maintaining and feeding countless life forms. The sea is a symbol of calmness. It has its qualities. Divers go to the bottom of the sea and take pictures during nature programs. The beauty beneath is incredible. We are amazed at the scenery. The views are totally out of this world. We are damaging it by polluting it and endangering the sea life forms.

Birds live in their world and are very close to nature, as they are free to move from one tree to another when the animals live on the ground and are subject to human dictates. Birds teach us, complete detachment. They lay eggs in the nest, hatch them and feed the young ones until they fly. Once the young ones are ready to fly, they leave the nest or the elders push them over to find their life course.

We, as humans, want to control our young ones and don't want them to leave. In return, we become responsible for our suffering. God has given us the quality and strength to stay alone and survive. If we, with our superior capabilities, cannot survive, 'Then who can? We need to learn a lot from our flying friends.

Now we come to our ground and flying insects. Nothing is created without purpose. The ground ones are superior to us at home-building and teach us discipline. If you dare to watch them closely, everyone is a builder and a soldier right from the beginning. In comparison, we are lazy and useless. The flying ones, such as butterflies, provide beauty, while honey bees provide honey and many others spread pollen; otherwise, there would be no vegetation.

Nobody likes mosquitoes because they feed on polluted filth and pick up deadly poisons that they inject into the human body. No one is safe. They teach us how dirty we are and how much filth we produce. If they live on the usual grounds, they won't be as deadly as now.

The greenery is incredible around us and the trees are beyond description. We love to walk in their presence, as we feel calm and peaceful. The tree is a symbol of life and it releases oxygen for us to breathe. Everything in this world moves and fights. They teach us patience. They grow and have their being in one place and never complain. We can do any overt act against them but they never complain or fight back.

As a gift, they produce fruit for us to feed on and we sit under their shadow when tired. They are part of our planet's natural beauty. We are destroying them to produce furniture, which is artificial decoration. Our selfish desires will never end. The result is a big hole in the ozone layer and destructive climate changes.

In England, the temperature has risen by two degrees Celsius within the last forty years. If this rise of two degrees continues every forty years, we will experience catastrophic results. We are human beings; we must adopt the qualities of a tree.

We must pay attention to nature and let them have their existence as we have ours. We depend on nature more than it depends on us. Earth, air, water and fire are the backbone of our lives; It is the basis on which we live. We can never count the life-forms on this planet and they are all created for a purpose.

We all experience it in our way. We are not allowed to interfere in the ways of nature. Nature takes its course. We must learn to let it be. Hatred is the killer of love. We must learn to love and give love unconditionally. We must carry universal thoughts and have a love for all life. By attaching yourself to one religion or country, you are limiting yourself. You must love every particle, atom and drop of life; otherwise, you will never become universal.

Without this love for all life, God-realisation is not possible. Self-realisation is becoming aware of yourself as a soul.

The 'within factor' and God-realisation can answer the question, 'What is the soul? You become complete within yourself. We all are the same and our goals are the same; our approaches may differ slightly.

No saint or prophet has claimed that there are two Gods. 'If we know God is one, when will we realise that we are one? Love thy neighbour as thyself and love all life. In return, God will love you. You are near and dear to it and you have been found wanted.

# ABORTION

Abortion is regarded as a sin by most religions. A few years back, the rate of abortion was high and at present, it is stabilising; it is becoming a global concern. It is becoming a way of life to abort whenever it suits the needs. In the Western world, this takes place for many reasons. Pregnancy takes place out of wedlock or the number of single mothers increases, especially in European countries. Most couples do not agree to have children and some cannot afford one.

In the East, people are hesitant to have too many girls. If the scan results show the gender of the baby is female, it is most likely that abortion will take place. At that point, religion is forgotten and mental satisfaction is the primary concern. There is no answer for what is happening in the East but prevention is better than cure in the West.

'Is abortion a sin? It is believed to be a sin by many religions because we have killed a future human being. Each religion has different beliefs. Those religions do not believe in reincarnation; it should not matter to them. Some religions believe that the soul enters the mother's womb when pregnancy occurs. Others believe that the child's body grows in accord with the internal system of the mother and as soon as the birth takes place, the soul enters the body and the child's first cry is evidence of that.

Every person has the right to believe as they wish. In the past, people were more religious and did not believe in abortion. Initially, the sexual union was to have a family. Nowadays, sex is used for pleasure and it is explored from every angle possible; this is why pregnancies occur for no reason. The theory of reincarnation states that the soul is created and works off karma. It is decided by the lord of karma where it will be born before the pregnancy occur.

Birth is based on the existing karma and the family it is related to, providing the best experience for the soul. The family, other relations and all situations must fit as the glove fits the hand. The pregnancy takes place and the child is born. Regarding both views, it does not matter if the soul has already entered the new body or will enter at the time of birth. In both theories, one point is common; Pregnancy occurs because the soul has decided to have its future in this family.

So, in either case, the child's body is in the process of growth and after approximately nine months, it will take birth and the soul will begin its new experience. Now, if we abort this body due to our physical wishes or circumstances, we have changed the destiny of that soul, which initially has chosen this body and this particular family to work off its karma. The soul cannot go to any family to have this experience because everything is based on karma.

Therefore, aborting a child halts the journey of the soul. It has to wait for another similar opportunity to arise in the same family. Under any circumstances, no one kills the soul. The soul never dies and neither does it sleep, as we hear in some mythological stories which contradict their religions. There are many stories but I will illustrate one here. A lady was pregnant and a saint came to give some instructions to her.

They were meant for her future child, who was in her womb because that child was a special soul and had to perform special duties in life. This young person was performing his duties, which were tricky and challenging. He completed the task to a point and then he got stuck. The myth says that when the saint was giving instructions to his mother, she fell asleep.

This young man could only perform his duties up to the point when his mother was awake and able to take instructions. As soon as his mother slept, he did not recall what the saint had told her. This will never be true. If the mother had slept physically, this would have had nothing to do with that child's experience. First of all, if the mother had fallen asleep, this would have been possible, as we all sleep from time to time but the mother's soul body was awake.

The experiencer is the soul, not the physical body. Also, we have noted that when a woman is pregnant, especially in the later months, just before the child's delivery, the mother is often sleeping as usual but the child inside the womb is moving. You can notice this during every single pregnancy.

So, we conclude that if the mother fell asleep, this would not necessarily mean the child was sleeping. Therefore, all these mythological stories are contradictory and baseless but they are fascinating to hear. However, when you sit down and try to analyse them, you will likely find them inaccurate. I am more awakened as a soul when sleeping physically.

Often, the baby dies before its physical birth occurs while still inside the womb. This could be due to a malfunction of the mother's biological system, as it could not nourish the child's body; the child turns blue and dies. It may be due to spiritual reasons, although this happens very rarely. If the soul is not happy with the future family, it can refuse to enter this newborn baby. If this is the case, the baby will be stillborn. The soul is a free entity.

It can change its wish if it does not want to enter a particular body or family. This can only happen if this soul has a very light karmic pattern. In most circumstances, when the child is born, it already has very heavy karmic ties with its particular family. The soul has no choice but to take birth and work off karma with its family and experience; childhood, youth, middle age, old age and eventually death.

Abortion is condemned in Christianity. The Bible states that the deliberate taking of an innocent human life breaks the sixth commandment; 'Thou shall not kill.' It is also condemned in Sikhism as an instruction; 'Jiv-hatya' means 'Do not kill.'

It is also not allowed in most world religions. If we study phrases such as 'Thou shall not kill' and 'Jiv-hatya, ' we see that they refer to human killings and killings of any kind where a soul is involved. We, as human beings, have superior intelligence. We take every situation for granted. 'Is abortion a sin or not? When we abort a child, we are changing the soul's destiny. 'Is this sin? The answer is within. We are all sinners.

We need to think twice before we take any action. We are responsible people but our wrongdoings are the cause of suffering in this world. Do not create any bad karma which you cannot quickly pay. 'God's mill grinds slowly but it grinds exceedingly well,' they say. You are the Master of your life, do not live your life with your eyes closed; the pitfalls are many waiting to trap you. Divine light and sound are there for your guidance. Let the Spirit flow and you can never go wrong.

# MARRIAGE

Marriage occurs when karmic patterns from the past and the present blend together. It is the destiny of two people involved in matrimony. They are working off their old karmas, which have brought them together and new karmic ties will be in action as life goes along. It is not just the karmic pattern of the bride and groom but also the two families and families close to them. The bride and groom are not only working off karmas but establishing a new pattern of karma as they become parents.

Living with parents, we are on the receiving side in our younger years. Since we are parents, we moved to the giving side. This is good; you must learn to give and not to receive. This is the secret of getting off the Wheel of Eighty-Four. Otherwise, this is continuous and we are moving along with it. As long as we have karmic ties, we will be involved in the Wheel of Eighty-Four. The most substantial karmic pattern is between husband and wife.

As long as this karmic pattern is strong, the marriage will take place, which is the destiny of two people. This cannot be avoided even if we try. If a marriage is purposely avoided or broken, this can jeopardise karma, so you must meet again under the same conditions in future lives. Under challenging situations, you must remain patient and go through the experience. All the difficulties are the result of heavy or severe types of karma.

It is your past creation. If the karmas are balanced, life will also go smoothly. The success of your marriage is based on compromises with each other. There is a continuous contribution from each other. One-sided friendship does not last very long; the relationship will begin to dry up and starve. Only saints can run their lives very smoothly. If married life runs more smoothly than expected, this can be dangerous or a blessing in disguise.

It may be because very few karmas are left between the couple and physical action comes to a standstill. They begin to drift away from each other. They leave each other with free will and there is no love lost between them. They will remain friends and send goodwill to each other. This type of departure is very smooth and healthy. Divorce that ends in courts and quarrels is very dangerous, especially for the children.

As they say; the doings of parents often visit upon the children because they have to suffer the consequences of their parents' wrongdoings. Then the children are bound to suffer at the hands of destiny. The godly love provided by both parents won't be there. One parent's love is available most of the time, even in a diluted form.

The responsibility of one parent increases and that parent fails to give full attention to the infant or adolescent. This will reflect on the child's character, reflecting upon their children later in life. Living with a new partner, your child's step-parent, could be another disaster, as they could be suffering at the hands of their step-mother or father. It is another grave experience.

Many parents turn a blind eye to the situation for selfish reasons. These parents are not very responsible and are dangerous to their society. They can create havoc. Children under these circumstances become mentally disabled and lose their self-confidence and a fear factor builds up in their auras. Marriage is a big responsibility and it should not be taken lightly. The ritual should not be performed for convenience.

This is the downfall of the whole situation and many more to come. Marriage is a very healthy process for working off karma. At the same time, it is a very beneficial spiritual experience for the soul to unfold and attain maturity to become an assistant to God. Marriage within the family, which occurs in a few religions and is permitted by the elders, has many side effects.

The karmic patterns have been built enormously over the centuries or millennia and it is more challenging to get them out of the system. These are usually marriages of convenience. It is most likely that cousins will marry cousins. Even from childhood, they know who is made for whom. The parents don't have to go too far to look for the boys or girls for this purpose. This is a straightforward system but the results are not very healthy.

If people within the same blood group marry, it brings down the activity of blood cells. This leads to ill health in general and disabled children. Forced marriages are a total disaster, setting up a battleground for the rest of their lives. The parents are responsible for this. Nowadays, people are more aware of this and marry outside if possible. This awareness will make a person think twice before getting involved with close families.

Eventually, this system is going to break up soon. The marriages within the community are very healthy and prosperous, as the couple will have the same background and language. Apart from the love factor in their lives, they can share communal topics and the future marriages of their children will be pretty easy. Marriage outside the community is now standard practice.

It can be very successful; if problems creep up for any reason, there is no reason for the community to intervene. On the other hand, communities and families intervene and most likely; they will find a solution. When love dry-up and there are very few reasons in common to carry on, having children can ensure the success of the marriage. The parents will not part as quickly as the children are now the focal point.

Marriage is an excellent system that helps humankind live in a civilised way. If in the future, this system fails, it could lead to worldwide disaster. 'If all men and women stayed single, could you imagine what the future would be like? Marriage can occur between man and woman, provided they are willing to take responsibility.

**Islam**: The consent of the boy and girl is asked. The words 'Kabul hai' (meaning accepted) are repeated three times if they agree. Then the mullah (priest) declares this couple to be married.

**Christianity**: The bride and groom take the vows in the presence of a priest and at the end, they speak, 'We do.' They are pronounced man and wife.

**Sikhism**: The couple sits in front of the holy book (Guru Granth sahib) and four lavas are read by the Giani (priest). Marriage takes place in the presence of their parents and a respected community. These four lavas explain their physical and spiritual life as a couple; to appear as two but act as one for life.

**Hinduism:** The couple takes saat-phere; in this ceremony, the couple circles around the fire seven times while the priest recites religious verses. Their marriage takes place in the presence of parents and respected community members.

As you can see, each religion has its way of expressing that a couple is married. This proves that it does not matter how it is said or done. It is the acceptance of responsibility that counts and it is for life.

Marriage is for life.

# WILL I EVER BE HAPPY?

As long as we live in the lower worlds, the answer will be 'No.' We live in the worlds of matter, energy, space and time. We will never be happy as long as we are subject to material planes. Every person in the world is looking for peace and happiness; they will never find it. The negative force has to keep us trapped in problems. You try to work out one problem and say, 'I will be happy after this,' but you will find two or more problems already springing up to take its place.

So, it is a never-ending process because people do not try to work out their bad karma. Instead, we are willing to create more to eliminate the first problem. This way, we are always on the move, creating more and more karma until we do not know where to turn to. There is nothing that will give us happiness. Some people are poor and unhappy because their needs are never met. Then there are people with lots of money who are unhappy because their problems extend from having money.

A poor person will never know that money cannot buy happiness. Mahatma Buddha was born a prince. He had all he could ask for on a material basis but he was not happy. People with children are not happy because of problems related to the children. Those people who have no children are not happy because they have none. Mahatma Buddha said, 'The cause of suffering in this world is our desires.'

So, the critical point is to try to have as few desires as possible. This can reduce our problems. Whatever you have in life, feel content and feel; It is more than we require. This feeling can overcome many hurdles in life. No one can give you happiness; you have to work on your weaknesses. Anger can cause many problems. Someone may irritate you so much that you feel like hurting them. However, 'How many people can you hurt? Another one is ready to take its place, probably around the corner. Stay in balance.

Following spiritual teachings or a Master will not give you instant happiness. Sometimes we feel that we are going through more problems than before. This may be true. The Master will not provide you with instant happiness because he knows how to lead you to happiness. Upon meeting with the Master, he will begin to work off your bad karmas, sometimes very quickly, if he knows the Seeker can withstand the pressure.

This will lead you to a fair amount of happiness or spiritual understanding in the future.

This will help you to face the problems in a balanced manner. The problems may still be around but they do not bother you because you have become spiritually strong. During the early meeting with the Master, people get frustrated and say; we came here to seek happiness but suffer more than before and many will leave.

Pseudo-masters always try to give you instant happiness. They don't want to lose you like good salespeople, as you are their good customer. As long as the income continues, they will tell you every good and happy story in the book. This will work for the short term; eventually, the stories will fade away, as they were baseless. When we build giant castles without good foundations, we know the result. People will end up in despair.

When this happens, you begin to shop around from Master to Master and one day, with good karma, you find the Master according to your unfoldment. All the happiness in this world is temporary. True happiness lies within; we are always searching for it externally. On the outer, we face obstacles because our senses create situations and act accordingly. We are negative, trained to be negative, so we must face this negativity.

If we train ourselves to go within, into the subjective worlds, we will find peace. The flow of Spirit is the feeling known as the 'bliss state.' Upon coming out of this bliss, we feel better and this is the food for the soul, mind and body. Overall, this inner visit leaves us with a feel-good factor and we feel better for days. Those who manage to have this experience each day are the blessed ones. This is possible through regular spiritual exercise. When we are successful, we call this 'dying daily.'

This is the first and final resort to finding peace. The attempt to go within must be successful; we often notice that our imagination is busy with mental problems. Many imaginative fights materialise and we create lots of karma. A negative thought during meditation can multiply manyfold. You must be in a free and relaxed mood. This is very important; otherwise, you could end up on the scale of loss when we attempted to gain.

This is why many saints sit in meditation for hours to feel this bliss state. They often help needy people by travelling to them and solving their problems. As you know, people cry out for help every second when their faiths don't help. These travellers reach out and wipe their tears. This does not happen every day and in every place because there are only a few saints capable of helping while there are millions of people asking for help each day.

This world remains intact because of these few assistants of God. Nowadays, most people and governments are trying to destroy this world and they have no interest in creating peace. In the name of peace, more destruction is done in the background. Most people who have no experience do not understand the mission of these saints. If you can adopt even the slightest ability of these beings, of what they know and their bliss state, that will make your life a lot easier and more peaceful.

Be yourself and let the others be. Allow everyone to have their own psychic space and in return, you may remain happy forever.

# SECURITY

The whole world aims to have some security, providing peace of mind. This is the feel-good factor. We all strive and say, 'If I have this much, my worries will be over' or 'I can survive on that.' To own property and money are means of providing security. We educate our children for the same purpose to achieve security for themselves in the future. We work hard physically and guide our children to do the same.

It is not a wrong thought. Ask within; 'Is this enough or do we need more than this? As Jesus Christ said, 'Man cannot live on bread alone.' By this, he meant that we need more than world securities. There are two main types of securities; physical and spiritual. We mainly concentrate on physical security because we are physical. We cannot see beyond; therefore, we spend most of our life achieving as much as possible.

Upon death, we leave it all behind for our children to carry on with the same task. We must pause and ask ourselves, 'Was this effort worth it? 'If so, what did I achieve out of it? If you think about it, you have gained nothing but found a toy for yourself to pass the time in this life. In a sense, the whole of life has been wasted when you could have earned inner or spiritual security at the same time as you did all your duties. If only someone had guided you.

Spiritual security is the actual security for the soul. The soul carries this security when it departs from this world. The basic process is; You begin to create good karma for yourself. You follow the spiritual path to educate yourself by whatever means, such as reading and meditation. This is the first step to opening up spiritually and becoming an awakened soul.

This is an easy task. It may take a short period or a lifetime to achieve proper spiritual security. You can start on this at any point in your life. There are no limits. As soon as you learn to balance your five passions of the mind, you are on the way to success. These five passions keep getting in your way and lead you astray from your real goal. They are the snares of illusion that play all its tricks to keep you grounded.

In today's world, 'lust' is on everyone's mind. Lust is expressed by attraction to the opposite sex. Nowadays, we are on the fast track. No one tolerates anyone else. Anger plays its part too. Material gain is on everyone's agenda; greed plays its role. After gaining everything in life, attachment to loved ones or overall attachment to anything becomes the 'I' factor (vanity), expressing the sentiment, 'I am superior to them all.'

It is difficult to become a spiritual person when you have all these attached to yourself through the mind. After much struggle, if you gain some spiritual ground, the 'I' factor intervenes and reminds you that you are doing something better than the others. To become a spiritual person, you must become humble. The humbler you are, the more outstanding your achievements in the spiritual world will be.

Humbleness is an attribute of God that comes automatically within saints. You need a living Master who can guide you and check your progress from time to time; if you are stuck, he will show you the way out. Otherwise, you are sitting in a class but not knowing your progress. When you leave the physical body at the time of death, 'Do you know what you have achieved? Or is it just guesswork to satisfy your mind; 'Yes, I have done enough and the Master will look after me in the other worlds,'

It is your imagination or belief that your Master will look after you, 'But you are not sure it will happen that way? If you are not sure, there is no guarantee it will happen according to your wishes. I will say to you, work hard if you need to but you should know who you are and where you are going after death before leaving this world. This can only be known; if you are capable of soul travel at will. Then you have examined the outcome. That is true and proper spiritual security.

All else is an illusion.

# PROBLEMS ARE ZERO

Nowadays, the world is acting as if walking in quicksand in many situations. The tempo of life is speedy and we are running in all directions to find peace. At the same time, we aim to possess whatever we can within our grasp and some things that are not even nearby. Due to this, we run into lots of problems. If this is our only aim, it is tough to find peace. When we try to grasp everything at once, we achieve nothing.

Most of the problems are our creation, resulting from our past errors. As they appear to us, we have to face them. Minor problems don't bother us as much but some situations take up so much mental energy that we become upset. The mental upset depends on the strength of the situation. We are not trained to face problems; this is a human weakness. We can handle it reasonably well if it is a happy occasion because we like happiness.

Even if we are not trained to handle happy occasions, we still manage well. Our gut feeling tells us that we will be fine. When it comes to problems, our capability is inferior. We get upset quickly and most people lose sleep over this. We can lose our appetite; if the problem is severe. We can have a heart attack, brain haemorrhage or terminal illness. At this point, we must ask ourselves, 'Was it worth; taking these problems so seriously?

'What is the problem? The problem is a situation that is not in your favour. At this moment, a problem may seem so severe that we cannot help thinking about it. **Equation:** Think of a problem you had last or the year before or five years ago. 'Do you recall the strength of that particular problem? Yes, indeed, it was very powerful at that time. 'Now ask yourself, does it bother you now, after five years? The answer is probably 'No.' Problems come and they die down and disappear altogether with time.

We have learned that problems are not permanent. They come and disappear with time and they are never heard of anymore. No problem can bother us if we understand this concept and build it into our system. It does not matter how strong it may be. I have concluded that make it zero from day one when a problem comes. Let it pass along. Do the best you can to resolve it. Don't let it bother you. With time, you are going to forget it anyway. Practice this. Success will be yours.

# THE REAL AGE OF HUMANS

Life is a gift from God for us to live and experience as we go along from life to life. We also travel within the cycles of life. There are a few different cycles set by time. One of them is five years, seven years and twelve years. The five-year cycle is relatively essential in human lives but the seven-year cycle is significant because it brings many changes. So, the sequence is seven, fourteen and twenty-one.

We should expect some changes in life as this seven-year cycle begins or ends. If you are going through a bad patch in life, work out your life and divide it by seven. You will know whether you are in the middle of a seven-year cycle or near the end. You should expect the change to bring you good or bad luck. This is the ancient theory; it will not apply to every person, especially those who follow a spiritual Master.

The Master helps the Seeker unfold spiritually; he purposely speeds up your karma. Some suffering is expected because the Seeker is taken out of the astrological system. The pundits use the astrological approach to forecast the future of anyone concerned. This theory means a lot to us, as we are concerned with our physical suffering, so we take it very seriously. The seven-year cycle has another significant influence on the soul as we go from life to life.

We will not discuss the lower lives of God's creation at this stage. Once the soul has progressed from the animal to the human level, it can make its final journey to achieve spiritual freedom. We must go through several lives to achieve this. When the soul progresses from the animal state to the human for the first time during this journey, it takes the male form. It is not as simple as that going from male to female.

Zodiac cycles have a significant effect on the purity of the soul. Each year, the weather and four-season change. The moon appears in different shades; it is never the same. Full or half-moon bring many changes in our physical lives, especially in the female form, as her hormones change. The male and female have to go through seven cycles to explore the influence of each star sign as an experience.

The soul will spend seven times twelve; eighty-four lives in the male form and the same time in the female form. Now you know where the Wheel of Eighty-Four derives its meaning. This is the minor cycle of eighty-four and counting other life forms into the total comes to eighty-four hundred thousand. Counting the number of animal life forms is a huge task. As we are on our final journey, we will discuss only the male and female human lifespans.

So, our journey as a soul is dependent on this cycle of eighty-four. Eighty-four lives are the minimum; it could be more. Nowadays, we do not spend our allotted lifespan of 144 years during each visit on the physical plane. It could take twice the number of lives to experience the full influence of each star sign. Over the centuries, the lifespan of humans has become very short due to many reasons, mainly the lifestyles we have adopted. The five passions of the mind also contribute to this trend.

We come to another cycle for twelve years; our physical lifespan is based on this. Several other theories are based on the number twelve (accounting for the fact that there are twelve hours in half a day, twelve months in a year). If you sit down and spend some time on this, you will be surprised to learn how many twelves we depend on. Many of the spiritual scriptures are written based on twelve chapters.

Our lifespan cycle is twelve years. According to ancient theory, each person has to complete twelve cycles in one lifespan. A lifespan is one cycle of twelve years, times twelve complete cycles, equal to 144 years. This is the proper allotment of time from birth till death. It could be more in special cases, such as the lives of saints or some yoga practitioners. In most cases, the opposite is true.

This is due to our lifestyles, resulting in sickness and very high stress, which is the killer of the physical body. Most avenues lead us to a shortened life but make the most of it while experiencing it. The gift of life is to live, do not destroy it. Life is so precious but short; the time is slipping through our fingers so fast. Everything seems to be out of control.

Many people have plenty of time but, due to a lack of spiritual awareness, let their time go down the drain without making much use of it. I will demonstrate a small calculation to draw your attention to the number of productive days you have in your life. If a person lives for a hundred years, this will equal 100 x 365 = 36,500 days. At present, the average lifespan is seventy-five years, equal to 27,375 days.

The first twenty-five years will be taken out from birth to finish your education which is 9,125 days. The age of 26 to 60 years will be your productive working or quality time. Now the number is 35 times 365 = 12775 days. Most people want to hang up their gloves from working life, if possible, at 60 years. From age 60 years, our health has been on the decline. Now, I do not want to shock you but out of 12775 productive days, we have not taken out the weekends or bank holidays.

I will leave that part for you to work out. Now you see that you have no control for more than half of your lifespan. Now you know what a short time we have and much more to do. We cannot afford to waste a single day. Make every day productive from onwards. I am sure you are going to make the most of your time.

This is your life.

# TERRORISM

The suffix '-ism' is always related to some religion. Terrorist groups are seen in all countries, with many followers. It seems to be a way of life for some religions, in an era when we should be living in civilised societies. The reasons are many for all these activists. No reaction comes without a cause. Any person in this or any universe has no right to dominate or occupy anyone's psychic space without prior permission of the occupant. There are two ways of entering someone's psychic space, legally or illegally.

This will apply to a person or a nation; the spiritual law is the same. To enter another country legally is referred to by the law as UNO and upon their entry, we call them soldiers. When other people make the same entry but illegally, we call them terrorists. The fact is, neither of them should be there in the first place. They both hold weapons in their hands. To justify the weapons of destruction by both sides have many reasons.

When you take a close look at the lives of soldiers or terrorists, you will notice they are both innocent parties. Governments or terrorist groups activate the motivation behind them. Then, destruction occurs and the victims are always innocent civilians who have nothing to do with either side. This craze of terrorism plagues all countries. I would not be surprised if, one day, this took the shape of an international religion.

Many groups claim to be part of this or that religion today. According to their spiritual scriptures, terrorism does not exist as far as any religion is concerned. Otherwise, it cannot be a religion. I am not a politician, nor have I ever been, nor will I ever be. Politics do not interest me and I have never voted for any government. You are either a spiritual man or a politician. You cannot be both. This is a straightforward mystery but people failed to solve it.

You fail to decide whether you are a religious person or a politician. You will notice that you are neither and your lifespan comes to an end. I am not a terrorist, nor have I ever been, nor will I ever be, as violence does not interest me. It is totally against the spiritual law. Violence disobeys the will of God, as I mentioned in the chapter, 'Love All Life.' All religions forbid killing. Some religions may not agree about killing animals but we all agree that killing humans is forbidden.

This agreement is not up to my standards but I do not expect the same from all. I am aware of the First and Second World War history and many more wars have taken place since. India and Pakistan have fought a few battles between them since 1947. The Soviet Union is shattered into pieces. Muslim countries are at constant war with each other. America is constantly at war with some country, at least one at any time. They have their explanation to justify their actions.

I still remember the days of the Vietnam War in the 1960s, when children were born inside the manmade tunnels (Cu chi tunnels) and grew up in those tunnels to become soldiers. Very few countries have managed to stay out of war since World War II. 'Can you imagine the number of humans who have died or been killed by each other? The number is in the hundreds of millions. 'Can anyone show me statistics that indicate this country or that country has gained from all these wars?

The conclusion is that we have lost to each other. We have lost our loved ones for no reason. The amount of finance we have drained on weapons that could have been spent on our countries to make better places to live and enjoy life as a whole. Poverty would have vanished long ago. The countries at constant war are responsible for bringing poverty into their countries and future generations have to pay the price. Your present actions will depend on the kind of life you want to create for future generations.

'Do you want your children to become beggars or live lives of luxury? It is for you to decide now. Governments have their way of justifying their attacks on other countries; this is merely blaming each other. A general characteristic of countries is secret services, better known as spies. Almost all countries today have spies but when they are caught unexpectedly or cause terrible damage, the media springs into action and blows everything out of proportion.

As I have said before, the victims are always innocent people in every situation. These innocent people trust their governments, looking for an answer but it is hardly ever given. They lose hope and the trust they have invested and as a result, terrorists are born. They form small groups and take the law into their own hands. They have training grounds and are thoroughly trained to the same level as military commandos.

When they take charge of any mission, they come fully loaded with all the weapons they can carry. 'But at the end of their mission, do you know they all die? Following this mission, the innocent victims become future terrorists. 'Will this ever stop? 'Do you know why these terrorists die while on their mission? It is very simple; because they are not politicians. Many governments create terrorist attacks to win elections over the opposite party within their own countries.

Many cause grievous damage to their loved ones to gain sympathy votes. This is the game of power. It can take the individual to any level, no matter how degrading it can be to achieve their goals. Every violent situation creates terrorists all through the world and when the person acts like a terrorist, at that point, they belong to no religion, whereas before, perhaps they were. All these religions agree that we humans carry the spark of God within us, known as the soul, which is God itself.

If we understand that all humans are mini-gods, if we kill one or many of them, can we ask ourselves the question, 'What is my religion? The answer will be negative. God has given you life and the ability to analyse yourself to seek answers. Governments and other groups play the game and in return, innocent people become puppets and victims. The world needs to become more responsible and make this a better place to live. May God be with you, whatever religion you believe in.

May peace be with you.

# SOUL MATE

The search for a soul mate with whom to get friendly or marry is most common among humans. Some are happily married and there are a few whose marriages are unsteady. The latter have the impression in their minds that their married life is unsteady because they are mismatched and not soul mates. That is why they cannot get along with each other. Even though they are married, mentally, they are still looking for their soul mate.

This epic of great search is going on throughout the world, regardless of people's religion. The race is on. Now the question is, 'Will they ever find it? There are many reasons why people find difficulties in their marriage. It could be the karmic pattern they are going through at the moment. Some of the karma is very disturbing and will make your life hell. We need to work off these karmas at some point in life because they are very upsetting.

'Do you know it was karma that brought them together as a couple in the first place? Due to this working off, we moan and groan and the marriages break up in the middle of this process. If the experience is not complete, we have to go through it repeatedly. If all the karmas are worked off, this could be another reason for separation.

The search for a soul mate depends entirely on the soul's journey in the lower worlds. Soul mates are so close to each other. For spiritual reasons, soul mates cannot put their hands on each other. This is done for the soul's experience as it enters the worlds below the soul plane. The soul in the soul plane is pure Spirit yet individual. Every soul is part of the Ocean of Love and Mercy but retains individuality.

The soul's journey into the lower worlds has to experience the opposite factor in all creation exists. The soul becomes subject to positive and negative. The soul itself is neuter or pure Spirit and has no gender, male or female, similar to its creator God. The soul takes its embodiment through male and female forms in the early stages of life, from plants to birds to mammals and it does not bother us much.

As we progress to the human level, we become more aware of our feelings and want the circumstances to match our requirements. These circumstances make us believe that there is someone in the world who will be my life partner. This belief is like putting oil on fire and we make many mistakes, such as adultery and divorce. The truth is that as the soul attaches to both male and female forms to work off its karma, it takes the male body's shape and may take the female form next time.

It does not have to follow the order of 'one male or one female. It could be a few males or a few females; it depends on the zodiac cycle and what zodiac influence the soul is working on. As the soul is **subject** to male and female forms, while the soul resides in the male form, it searches for its other half, the female factor. It is the same when the soul resides in the female form; it searches for its other half, the malefactor. This is why males are attracted to females and vice versa.

The soul is neuter but attached to male and female factors for its unfoldment. Therefore, it is searching for its other half (male or female), which is so near yet out of reach.

This creates an urge within us to look for it. As the saying goes, 'Curiosity killed the cat.' Finally, the soul does meet its counterpart as it progresses through several lives, works off all the karmas, gains experience and prepares itself to become an assistant with God. Then it is ready to leave the lower worlds, as it has earned spiritual freedom.

The soul enters the soul plane as a pure Spirit on its final journey. The male and female aspects merge once more to become neuter with full experience. Now the search is over. It was not the search for the soul. Soul itself was and is complete. It only came downwards for schooling. The mind and its five passions make us believe one thing over the other and lead us astray.

Another common problem is picked up in the media daily. Some male persons feel they are females and some think they are likewise trapped in the wrong body and should have been males. As explained in the chapter 'The Real Age of Humans,' the soul goes through each zodiac cycle to feel and experience the influence of that particular cycle. When people have mixed feelings, they are on the border of some experience from male to female or vice versa.

This is nothing new. The feeling of being trapped in the wrong body and soul-searching for its other half has always existed. In reality, there is no such thing as a soul mate but on the mental level, to have a better and more successful life, it is helpful to look for someone who has similar qualities and interests to yours. This will build up a better understanding as a couple. If you want to call this a soul mate, you may.

# WHO IS VEGETARIAN?

This is one of the most common questions asked by many religious followers. There is no dictate to anyone's way of living, as some religions allow eating meat openly. For example, Islam allows the eating of meat. Christianity allows fish on Fridays, as the earlier followers of Christ were fishermen. Sikhs were permitted to eat meat in the early days, during the crisis times when they were at war with Islam.

The only survival factor for them was the jungles. The times were so hard they used to sleep while still on the saddles of their horses. The attacks from the opposite were expected at any time. Under these circumstances, if everyday food was not available, the guru permitted eating meat. Otherwise, Sikhism is also against the taking of life for pleasure. This pleasure is related to one of the five passions of the mind (Kam).

Most religions do condemn the taking of life. In Christianity, one commandment is 'Thou shall not kill.' People take it very lightly; they believe it means not killing another human being. The commandment generally conveys the message for all life forms, apart from the vegetable world.

The practice of Jainism is the other extreme. They are totally and openly against the taking of any life forms. They are so serious about the subject that they wear small masks to cover their mouth and nose area, lest they kill even the germs in the air. We are not here to kill microscopic lifeforms but if they have to die that way, as we are breathing them in, then this is nature's way.

Nature plays a central part in our lives in telling us who is vegetarian, non-vegetarian or both. Nature has created life forms that are permitted to eat meat, their primary means of survival. They are given the means to kill and eat other life forms. For example, lions, tigers, hyenas, dogs, cats and others you can think or know of all possess a set of teeth. Most of their teeth are flat but two on the top and two on the bottom are longer.

These are known as incisors or fangs and they are used to bite the flesh of other animals, so we can call them non-vegetarian. A vegetarian is classed as any form with a set of teeth that are more or less flat. These flat teeth are adapted to eat plants. Humans have flat teeth but are overly clever and try to create many theories to win arguments to the contrary. We humans are not able to kill animals as the cat family does. We can eat meat when it is cooked in such a way that it becomes edible.

Many vegetarians are not as clever as we are, so they have to settle for what they are; cows, buffalos, horses and so many others. 'Have you ever seen them hunting? No, they eat only vegetation, as they are supposed to. There is much strength in vegetable food; they are stronger than us. That is an example to follow. In practice, humans give special feed to cows to increase their milk production.

This feed contains bone particles of animals, which are ground into powder and mixed with vegetable-based food. The result is what we hear in the news, such as mad cow disease. If we feed ourselves with something not natural or acceptable for our body structure, then catastrophic results are inevitable. This will get worse in the future. Nature has designed a third kind of creature, omnivores, to eat vegetables and meat.

Any life form with a beak to pick up their food, such as peacocks, crows, eagles, hawks and others, can eat seeds and hunt birds, mice, rabbits, snakes or fish from the ocean. These birds are designed to eat either way. There are no dos and don'ts. It is an individual choice but I have tried to explain the course of nature. We are not here to win any argument. It is up to the individual to follow their inner dictates.

'What difference does it make if we eat meat or vegetable forms of life? It is explained in the chapter called 'Karma.' To know more, read that chapter. Any food we eat creates karma. Seeds are on the lower karma scale and vegetation is next in line. Birds and followed by animals. The killing of humans is known as the biggest sin a person can commit. This is why we take it so seriously.

All other sins are taken for granted. I will leave it for you to decide what you want to eat. It is your decision that counts.

# SAINTS

A 'saint' is a person who maintains a high state of spiritual consciousness. As we enter such a person's presence, we feel spiritually blessed. A glance at his face will bring peace to our lives. The word saint is not a physical title for anyone to have. The saints work hard to achieve spiritual realisation; it is their love for God. God is so near and dear to their heart that they spend all their lives fulfilling its command.

Saints are very active people. Many people class them as passive when they don't know the subject. Saints hardly sleep. Their average sleeping time is between two to three hours and the rest of the time; they are so busy it is beyond belief. They are doing physical duties to attend to their followers to provide answers. Otherwise, many come for a glimpse.

During this 'glimpse,' they receive the gaze (tawega) of the Master, which is spiritual food for them and can last for a long time. Also, during this gaze, if the Seeker brings a question to the Master, it can be answered without exchanging a single word. I am witness to this myself. During a handshake, the look of the Master directly into your eyes will reveal the answer to your question. This is inner communication.

The answer is given and the receiver is delighted with the response. This is a miracle in itself. You do not do miracles to please people. They just happen. This is the way Spirit works. There is not a single saint in the whole of history with whom or his presence; miracles did not happen. Otherwise, their name would not be recorded in history today. This is how they became famous. Otherwise, they would have come and gone without a trace.

Saints show us direction and how to lead a good life. They are an example to us. Nowadays, the saints are the only means; we connect with the inner or nature. Saints attend spiritual seminars and thousands come to hear the word of God. The time spent in their presence can mould the direction of our lives. Saints have other duties, although they may seem passive by sitting in the same posture for hours.

People all over the world are crying out for help. Distance is no problem. To cut down this distance, they travel in subtle bodies to the other side of the world in seconds. This way, they can reach unlimited people in no time. In utter emergencies, they also direct projection if the situation requires it. If you know how busy they are, you would be astonished. Saints travel with followers into the inner planes.

At the same time, they look after their welfare and protect their physical bodies. According to their spiritual unfoldment, he is the designer of each experience given to the follower. He creates and executes the situations with perfection so the Seeker can experience and gain the knowledge he requires to achieve unfoldment. He is also preparing many other saints under his umbrella; this is done without requesting anything. It is all for the love of God; they feel it is their duty.

In return, he may not receive anything physically but spiritually; he receives the blessings of God manyfold; that is all he values. The more he gives, the more he receives. This is the proper business and we must grasp this point; By receiving only one day, your bank account will dry up and your business will be closed. All saints are not the same. Their level of understanding and spiritual approach varies.

This is the journey in steps. He operates from the physical to above high and does spiritual duties to the best of his abilities. Saints live on the physical but in a detached manner. There is only one God but a few people are very near and dear to it. No one becomes another God but they are extraordinary souls and God sends them on a special mission.

It is the call of the time and they will sacrifice themselves to accomplish the mission. They have no love for their physical bodies. They look at it as a clay shell. It is very similar to changing our clothes every day without placing great value on the clothing. They are aware of their next mission and will get another body. We cry for our loved ones when they pass away because we cannot see the other side but the saints can see and live on both sides.

They most likely prefer to live on the other side of the border. When they do live on the physical, all they get is suffering. They do not give a damn about this suffering because they know it is only for the physical body and spiritually at peace. They enjoy suffering because they are on a mission; They are here to set examples for the good of the whole. The saint is very alone but not lonely, as the presence of God is always with him.

He is alone as no one else shares the same state of consciousness. He prefers to lean inwardly, at peace and have his day. Saints are the most peaceful people on Earth. They are detached from the activities of the lower worlds and teach the same. Saints have a love for all the creation of God but on an impersonal basis. That is the love of detachment. Saints do not see themselves as saints; they see themselves as the same as anybody else.

'Higher or lower status'; these words do not exist in their dictionary. The followers experience the difference and we give them respect accordingly. Saints have very high ethics. On TV, all religious personalities have the title of saint attached to their names but they are not saints. They more or less preach their respected religion and they use the holy book as an authority to put across their message.

The command of the dialects in use is impressive and people mistake them as for saints. Saints can use the literature available today but most likely, they will go within and give a direct message for the present time that will open up the way for the people. The saints I admire include Jesus Christ, Guru Nanak, Buddha, Kabir and Farid. The message they have left for us is outstanding.

Saints are many but they are not born every day, probably one child in a billion. They are rare but they do exist. Those who know them are fortunate and are blessed by God. Saints are the most peaceful and down-to-earth people in the world. Most of them are temperamental. If they do lose their temper, it will be brief to express their point, which is always for the good of the whole. As the saying goes, some people do not get the message unless hit on the heads with a club hammer.

Often, they do this purposely to keep the masses away. Otherwise, they are as good as any young child or as wise as any older man. Saints have unique characteristics and traits which only very few can recognise. Blessed are those who happen to be in their presence, know them and be under their spiritual cloak. All saints are spiritual giants with inner vision. When people or followers go in their presence, they notice that most of their questions are answered without exchanging a single word.

Saints are always on the move, internally or externally. They talk to the audience and are simultaneously busy with people on their way for a glimpse of the Master. There are two reasons for this; first, to provide spiritual protection as they are on their journey and second, to scan the individual's intentions for a visit. The scan reveals whether the person is coming for a glimpse or has some kind of burden to clear. The Master acts accordingly.

This scanning is very similar to an X-ray machine. X-ray machines are a replica of inner vision. Once the Seeker makes the entry, the Master knows what is bothering the Seeker. Usually, the problem is solved and answered instantly; otherwise, advice is given. Nothing is hidden from the visions of a saint. If nothing can be done, everything goes silent. Once saints have unfolded spiritually, it does not matter their background. They become universal in thought and action.

They are beyond any related terms in the physical. They see each soul as part of themselves. It does not matter what form the soul is in. They see the expression of God in each form and admire its presence. God expresses itself as a soul through the position of a doctor, lawyer, saint, thief and all the beasts or birds in the sky. They are all states of consciousness. Their physical character expresses the maturity of the soul. That is the difference between all of us. Otherwise, we are all souls.

The highest state of consciousness is a saint who has progressed spiritually to be close to God. The saint may not be able to see God directly but he can feel the presence of God constantly. How he expresses this presence to himself is again his way of communicating with God and dialogues occur. When we ask a question, the answer comes back in the same manner. Most likely, it is silent communication but it is apparent to each other.

This is the communication of a saint and his followers depend on it. The followers depend on the answers given by the saint and in return, the saint depends on the Spirit for answers. Any answer through this communication is true, pure and final. The saint always says, 'On my own, I do nothing. It is the Spirit that does the job.' They do not take any credit for it. Once they start taking the credit for themselves, their form becomes diluted and will not be as effective as it was.

This is the state of neutral living; they are neither for nor against anything. It is a state of pure bliss and they work very hard to maintain this state of consciousness. There are many snares of illusion to bring you down but a constant struggle takes place to prevent this from happening. With our efforts and the help of Spirit, we have no limits. In the world of God, everything is rightfully ours to have and has our being in it.

# ORACLES

Millions of people make pilgrimages to oracles, temples, gurudwaras, masjids and churches. Few oracles are still alive but the others are just history. Dargah Sharif is the place for Sufi saints. The Temples, gurudwaras, masjids and churches are the places for everyday prayers. Many people go to the Himalayan Mountains, as few places are still alive. There are only a few oracles in this world.

You may find mighty saints nearby these oracles. Most oracles are just memories of past saints and people go there to petition to fulfil their desires. These saints have done their duties and now gone on to new assignments. There is a belief that some oracles are still alive and some attendees hear their voices giving guidance. This is another way of fulfilling their desires.

There are other oracles in the area of the Himalayan Mountains. They are the waystations to other spiritual worlds. They are alive and controlled by the people in charge. They are holy people but regular visitors are not welcome in these oracles because they are all hidden from profane eyes. Even the saints, who are not very successful but manage to travel out of their bodies, just wander around. They do the screening and find out their purpose of visit.

They may let them in if they come with good intentions; otherwise, a spiritual shield allows no one entry. This reminds me of my childhood, the saint I used to visit. He was a very successful soul traveller and thousands of people came to pay their respects. Most people are just regular visitors who just come and go but a few come with severe intentions as they enter your psychic space. Then there is a sign or alert signal.

This saint used to do a psychic screening, which is very similar to X-ray machines. Through screening, he used to find out the purpose of their visit. If the visitor's intentions are good, the saint will help them; otherwise, he creates an imaginary situation for leaving or refusing entry straight away. People do come with very heavy karma. Sometimes they are best left alone and allowed to go through their doings.

I love the approach of Mahatma Buddha, which was very peaceful; be yourself and let others be. He taught that a great deal of attachment to material things results from our desires. Desire means asking or looking for something materialistic. Mahatma Buddha states that desires are the leading cause of suffering. How right he was. His message was to dwell above the state of desires so you can have spiritual attainment.

His main aim was that all his followers have the same state of consciousness as he did. I hope this is possible. This world would be a much better place to live in if it were. Hinduism is the largest religion globally and millions of people go to Hindu temples to pray to Kali Mata and other Deity gods. In the same way, they all have material desires or they want to get a cure for their physical ailments.

In return, they promise to attend the same place a few times to fulfil their desires. Most of the petitions are fulfilled, as it is believed that Kali Mata is still around and communicates with her followers or appears to them in their dreams. Taking a bath in the river Ganges is also believed to give purity and healing to the physical body.

You can have all the petitions, desires or physical healings fulfilled by being at home. That is to raise your vibrations to the level where Spirit listens and acts upon them if you are worthy of it. The masses need to visit temples and bathe in holy waters to fulfil their desires or solve significant problems but none of this will likely happen.

With your efforts, most problems will work out anyway, while a few will work out with your prayers. If the prayers are made sincerely at a particular place, they can materialise. You are reminded of God's presence by going to any spiritual place. Praying at that place helps to raise your spiritual vibrations to the point where Spirit intervenes and the desire is fulfilled.

Some people give credit to that place or guru and recommend others do the same. But if you can raise your vibrations at any place, the results will be the same. Every place is holy ground. All you have to do is realise it. But everyone cannot do this. So, it helps if you can visit temples and bathe in holy waters; these places are the booster factors in your success.

# SPIRITUAL SCRIPTURES

Spiritual scriptures are mainly known as holy books. The Bible for Christians, the Qur'an of Islam, the Bhagavad Gita of Hinduism and the Guru Granth of Sikhism, were written by gurus or their appointees. These scriptures are the lifeline for millions of people today. These great teachers passed away long ago but they have left this excellent knowledge behind for the people to follow.

These writings are not that anyone could write. These spiritual souls, known as Masters, had so much spiritual knowledge that their writings still puzzle the minds of well-educated people. However, they were written centuries ago. The Guru Granth is written four hundred years ago and is the youngest of all and the Bhagavad Gita is the oldest, a few thousand years old. All these Masters hardly had any education compared to the academic standards of the world today. But despite their basic education, they had knowledge of the beyond.

This esoteric knowledge is not available on bookshelves. It never has been and never will be. It is 'spiritual knowledge.' This spiritual knowledge is gained under the instructions of the Master. The Seeker has to go through tough tests to access this knowledge. This spiritual knowledge supersedes all the education available in this world. These holy books were written in this world but the wisdom belongs to the worlds above.

Those Seekers initiated by their Masters will have access to study in the higher worlds. The esoteric knowledge cannot be expressed in full detail due to a shortage of vocabulary. To describe the glimpse of the higher is totally out of the question. The experiences I have had with the help of my Master's, it would be difficult to explain if I wanted to do so in writing. I wouldn't know where to start or finish but you can go over it again and again internally and enjoy it.

It will stay with you for the rest of your life. This is your inner strength. I have written these experiences in my diary, including the time and the date they took place. All these Masters were travelling with me into the subjective worlds, known as the astral, causal, mental, etheric, soul plane and above. We were the regular visitors and met with the lords of each universe. Jot-Niranjan, Omkar, Brahm, Par-Brahm and Satnam Ji were the respective lords of these universes.

These past Masters let us know what these lords were called; otherwise, we would not have known. All these secret passages from one universe to another resulted from their effort. They must have struggled a lot in the beginning. In writing, Hinduism is the first in line to give this knowledge to the world, up to the mental plane. Brahm Lok has been here all the time since the construction of the lower worlds but the effort of Krishna and other saints before him brought this knowledge to Earth.

The soul plane is the fifth plane from this universe. Guru Nanak of Sikhism brought the teachings in writing up to the tenth plane, known as Anami-Lok. The evidence is recorded in the Sri Guru Granth, the holy book of Sikhism but it is possible he went further. The tenth plane or tenth door (Dasam-Dwar) is not the same. When referring to the

Dasam-Dwar, we only talk between the mental and the soul plane.

Anami-Lok is another five universes higher than the soul plane. These Masters made regular journeys and gained as much knowledge as possible. Then they expressed their experiences in writing. The vocabulary is foreign to us because they used the same terminology as above, as a substitute was not available. This is why people don't understand the puzzling nature of the text. Today's readers draw their conclusions about the meanings of the text.

If you want to understand, you have to raise your vibrations to the level of those Masters who expressed their experiences, which is not possible. Even if you do, the experience will be different, as these universes are so vast. So, you will never be standing on the same ground where they were a few thousand years ago, apart from a few familiar places. All the lords are still the same. The teachings you will get today from these lords will be according to the present time.

The teachings, given a few centuries or thousands of years ago, took place according to their time. The teachings are always pure and remain that way but a few points are not relevant today, as time and lifestyle change. Mainly, all the holy scriptures have been divided into three sections. Put all three together and the holy book will be assembled.

**First section:** is the personal experience of the Masters in the holy planes.

**Second section:** describes how the Masters witness this world. This writing is situational. Some extraordinary situations occur; they notice and recite spiritual dialogue according to what they have seen and felt. This is called situational bani or spiritual dialogue.

**Third section:** is the overall achievement of the saints. This is based on their daily state of consciousness. As they walk about and do their routine work, the spiritual pearls of wisdom appear on their inner screens. As they receive this wisdom, they write it down.

Now, let us look at the Bhagavad Gita, which was recited in the middle of a war called Mahabharat. This is where Sri Krishna teaches the great warrior Arjuna and gives him the lesson of spiritual awakening according to the situation of that time. Sri Krishna expressed what he already knew spiritually and the message he wanted to give to the world, as well as the duty of Arjuna in this situation. It is believed that if this holy book is properly read and understood, anyone can achieve spiritual freedom.

The saints of Hinduism have contributed to bringing spiritual knowledge in writing to this world. They are peaceful and law-abiding people. They have many centres worldwide where they teach meditation to achieve inner experiences.

Now, let us look at Sri Guru Granth, the holy book of Sikhism. The first word is 'Ikk-onkar'. This is where Guru Nanak tries to express the one and only God. Upon his experience, all he could say was 'Ikk-onkar.' This was the best expression he could give. 'What do people know today about what he saw or who he was? No one can imagine unless they have had the same experiences. 'However, will his explanation be the same? In other words, 'We have seen you but we cannot express you—you are so great and beyond our imagination.'

This is why Guru Nanak was the first to mention this word, 'Ikk-onkar' in the fifteenth century. This is the first word written in the Guru Granth and the rest of the writing is the praise of it. This word Ikkonkar indicates to me that he has gone beyond Anami-Lok. This holy book was assembled more than four hundred years ago by the fifth, Guru Arjan Dev Ji. The Sikh gurus are the best example for other religious leaders to show what ethics a guru should hold.

Guru Nanak taught that God is one and everybody is equal and there is no caste system. On this basis, they included the spiritual experiences of all the known saints of that time, such as Kabir, Farid, Namdev, Bhagat Ravidas and many more. The writings of these saints are outstanding. Even today, people want to lead their lives accordingly.

Mahatma Buddha (real name Siddhartha Gautama) was born a prince but chose to become a saint and received enlightenment while meditating under a tree. He taught that desires are the leading cause of most of our suffering. He was also instructed to follow the middle path, in other words, to stay in balance. His main message was to be peaceful. To do this, you should be yourself and let others be as well.

The Bible is another holy book, although Jesus Christ did not write it himself. The messages he gave to people of the time include the Sermon on the Mount and other very striking dialogues, such as, 'Come and follow me. Those who come to me will be lifted up' and 'I am always with you.'

A few years later, St. Paul, the founder of Christianity, gathered as much spiritual material as possible about Jesus Christ and his teachings and assembled the New Testament. Jesus Christ was an extraordinary person and he left many examples for us to follow. Christians hold a firm faith and are heartfelt people.

The Qur'an is another outstanding holy book. Mohammad is the prophet and it is believed that Allah revealed the Qur'an to Mohammad through an angel named Gabriel in approximately 610CE. Islam means 'surrender to God.' Makkah is their holy place and it is built near the place where Ismael kicked the sand and freshwater from the spring began to flow. Even today, fourteen centuries later, it is still going.

Muslims believe every word is written in the Qur'an; is the word of God. The message is the same; Every person is equal before Allah. Allah is the almighty God and Mohammad is his prophet. All these religions and their scriptures give the same message; God is one and every person is equal before God. So, all these saints had very similar experiences. That is why their expression is almost the same. I love all religions and they are very dear to me. One way or the other, from left to right and top to bottom, they are connected to me.

By condemning any religion, we cannot go very far. If anyone preaches that they are better than the other, that person has a lot to learn. Everyone is the same, except in their state of consciousness. All souls are the creation of God; the difference is in the awareness of its creator. The beggar, thief, doctor and saint are all souls but they differ in their consciousness.

With time, we all progress to higher states of consciousness. One day, with experience, the beggar or thief will be writing spiritual revelations too. Many times, these changes occur in one lifetime. All these saints who made their contributions to these spiritual scriptures were down-to-earth and straightforward people. They set examples for us to follow.

One day—you never know—you could be one of them. God wants every soul to achieve as high a state of consciousness as possible. As souls, we all have a high state of consciousness invested in us. God wants us to unfold ourselves spiritually and consciously become aware of its presence.

# RELIGIOUS BELIEFS

Some religions believe in worshipping statues, while others do not; I do not worship statues or recommend them. It is an individual choice and must be respected as such. We have no right to condemn anybody's belief. One day, I watched a TV program where a religious leader spoke against a religion that believed in statue gods. A 'believer in statue gods' approached him with a question about his religion.

He answered, 'If you remove all the statue gods and stories about Brahma, Vishnu and Shiva, that is my religion. It is the first and the last religion to be believed by all.' That is fine. If this person disagrees with the worship of statue gods, this does not mean that Brahma, Vishnu and Shiva do not exist. He is well versed in his teachings. I admire his memory and knowledge of other religions.

However, speaking out loud and being well versed in book knowledge does not make you superior to anybody else. I cannot remember many lines by heart. This does not mean I don't know anything. We all forget that God has created every person or individual. We all have our free will and choice to think, believe, act and follow what we feel is suitable. We cannot make or dictate anyone to do our ways.

God has created us individually; everyone will have an individual belief about God upon true awakening. Those who will be closer to the principles of Spirit will be near and dear to God. Each individual is no more or less in this world. We are all playing our roles. In the same way, no religion is higher or lower in this world. They are all playing their roles to teach the human race according to their consciousness.

Those religions that want millions of followers to join them are not very progressive; they are trying to kill individuality with their dictates. One day, people will be spiritually awake and all will have a mutual understanding of spirituality beyond religion. It will not be any of the dominating religions today. As I have said before, the world and universes are constantly changing.

No man or religion has the power to hold the situations according to their wishes. Many dominating religions will fade away by the end of this century and a few new ones will emerge. This will depend on what is on offer and the demand for future thought. The repeating of old stories is not good enough. People want to know the truth. If you can offer something new, that is fine; otherwise, they will move on.

The wind will blow for genuine Seekers. There are only a few true spiritual Seekers in this world. At present, the approach to God is of a material type. No person is saying to God, 'I want to be in your presence' or 'Please help me be part of your will' or 'I want to become an assistant of yours.' Instead, we ask for material gain, prosperity, good health and everything else you can think of on a material basis.

No one has time to think beyond their selfish needs. The world as a whole has been through mass poverty. Most countries are above the poverty level, while a few are still struggling to make ends meet each day. So, at the moment, their need is food, not God. Within this century, all countries will rise above the poverty level. Once your material needs are fulfilled, you can only think beyond yourself.

The day will come when we will think beyond ourselves. The avenues will be many, such as self-exploitation on the negative side or positive and neutering to become a true Seeker. If we find fault in other religions and dictate our superiority, we only show our weakness and non-tolerance. India is a country of many faiths and many cultures. All religions celebrate their auspicious days together with complete respect.

Mumbai is a great city and is the home to Bollywood. There is no doubt that much negativity is reflected in the movies, affecting the nation, especially the youngsters. During filming, I noticed one positive point; all actors belong to different religions in India. Each does their best to see the success of that particular movie. During the production, they work as a whole under the same umbrella.

There is a common umbrella of God for us and we all have the same right to sit under it and have our being together. No one has the right to be superior to anyone. In the eyes of God (physical expression), every single atom is the same; each part has its qualities yet retains its individuality. Christians wear a cross around their neck; they cross their heart to pray or give themselves good luck.

Muslims raise both hands to do 'Abadat (prayer) to Allah,' and they wear a small cap, which is part of their symbolism. A Sikh wears a turban and maintains his five Ks. This represents him to the world as a Sikh. Hinduism has many symbols, such as the janeu, a string worn around the body or a tilak (mark) on the forehead and they believe in many gods; there is only one God. We all agree on this principle.

One of the favourites of Hinduism is Ganesha, the elephant god. They believe that it brings them prosperity, happiness and peace in their lives. If they feel secure by following this, then so be it. Some people believe in snakes and rats. These are their beliefs and all these are states of consciousness. We have not yet come to the point where everyone can think and act individually.

If we try to find fault in religious practice, each religion might look odd compared to the others. These two words 'there and here' are very important for any truth Seeker. The term 'there' is for those who think of God as far away and out of reach. The term 'here' is for those aware of its presence everywhere and within each atom, it has created. In a true sense, we cannot name the Supreme Being other than IT.

Once we give a name to the Supreme Being, the Creator of everything, we are bringing limitations to it. It cannot be limited to any single word, such as God or Paramatma. Our elders used these words to express the masses to recite its name. Any teachings that bring it into limitation by a name are a religion. Any religion that does not believe in having a living Master is spiritually inactive as it does not wish to prosper further spiritually. Three principles of God; God, Spirit and Master.

Similarly, nature has three principles to fire; fuel, oxygen and spark. If one of them is missing, the flame of fire will extinguish. Likewise, all religious teachings are only alive as long as three are present. Otherwise, similar to the flame, it is a dead-end religion. There are many preachers in this world and most of them have big titles in addition to their names, such as Maharaj, Bhagwan, Bapu, Sri and Sri-Sri.

All of them are preachers, not saints. No one is God but one can be known as a representative of their respective teachings. I watched a religious program on TV one evening and a person appeared on the stage to express his story. He used forceful language and emotions of mind and body and the audience responded similarly. I don't know if they learned anything spiritually but much mental pressure was relieved during this process.

It is their belief in communication with the Spirit. Others practice negative power, known as black magic. In some tribes, it is known as voodoo-ism. This is what they have learned and this is all they know. With time, they will know more and beyond. It is their right to have their being in the creation of God. Negative, positive and neutral; all these qualities are here to create balance.

We cannot ignore these qualities as long as we are in the lower worlds. This term, 'lower worlds,' reminds me of those who do not believe in God or have any insight into it. They are not worth arguing with. Surely you can use this time positively and so can they. No one should be dictated to or convinced in any manner. Give your message to anyone willing to listen. After that, it is their free will to accept or reject it.

Do not try to change their destiny. It violates spiritual law and you will be the creator of heavy karma for yourself. Most people do not even know what they are committing each day. The fundamental spiritual law is to be yourself and let others be. Entering someone's psychic space without their permission violates spiritual law.

# SOUL TRAVEL

This chapter will discuss all the aspects of having a successful experience of soul travel. We will not succeed without a thorough study of the subject. All Seekers are excited to have this experience but do not know-how. We admire our religious prophets for their spiritual abilities but they never revealed the secrets of their success. I approached a few saints to know the truth. I received evasive answers.

I was disappointed with their attitudes. Maybe they succeeded the hard way, so they don't want to easily let it go. I promised myself that I would leave something in writing for the whole world. Soul travel is so easy yet out of reach. When we talk about soul travel, the **soul** is the centre point of our discussion. 'We should know what the soul is? It is a unit of God-awareness. 'Where is it and how to make it travel? Soul travel is based on your effort and knowing how to do a proper meditation.

**Spiritual exercises:** You must do your spiritual practices daily, two or three times, if possible. This is for newcomers and those who have been with the Master for some time. Spiritual discipline leads to successful soul travel.

**Sitting position:** You may sit in tailor fashion or on a chair or sofa. I prefer to sit in a tailor fashion, back erect and chin slightly up; the Crown-Chakra should align with your spine. Hands somewhere on your knees with palms up. Never strain yourself. Spirit enters through the soft spot and it flows through the spine to reach all chakras within the body.

**Breathing:** Breathing is important and must be done correctly at least ten times. You breathe in through the nose and exhale through the mouth in a lengthy way. At the same time, try to feel relaxed mentally and physically. Now begin to chant your holy **word** given by the Master as explained how to chant. Once you have mastered this idea, you are doing the exercise and are into a spiritual experience before realising it. Do this for a minimum of half an hour to one hour.

**Awareness:** The total of your activities and creativities is called awareness. As explained in the next chapter; becoming aware of your soul and the action required will lead to a successful experience. The place where you meditate must be calm and peaceful, without disturbance.

**Feel-good factor:** This is a combination of attitude and attention. **Attitude:** Set up a good mood for doing your spiritual exercises. Your mind is clear and calm. You don't have any big problems that bother you. These are all setbacks and will cause you to have mixed vibrations, both positive and negative. You will not settle down mentally to have the experience in this situation.

**Attention:** Narrow your awareness into a fixed focus. Spiritual experience will depend on the strength of your attention. You must channel all your thoughts into a singular focus. Attention is effortless but at times it can be tricky. You must know where to put your attention. Attention is focus minus effort; It is like being suspended. The inner door opens inwardly; you cannot push against it. The more you try, the more it will shut on you. Obliquely focus your attention on the screen if you want to see the Light.

**Soul:** is a unit of God-awareness. It is part of the Superior Soul or God but still retains individuality. The soul is the creator of every action and the experiencer. The soul is the leading player in this spiritual game. The soul's residence is our third-eye, which is the seat of the soul. The soul may be trapped inside the skull area. This applies to people who have heavy karma.

Their mind is overactive. In this situation, the soul's actions are passive and it has little chance to get out. It could be just outside the skull area and still controlling the physical body. It could be wandering a few miles away, having experiences and doing regular physical duties. Many people are unaware they are travelling because it is as natural as breathing.

**Light and Sound:** Light is knowledge. Without spiritual knowledge, we will not be aware of our travelling. Light is essential to see our path when we are travelling. All things in this world are manifest by sound but the image requires light. The soul uses its light to illuminate the path to clear the darkness during travelling.

Without sound, we could not travel. Sound waves are moving inwardly and outwardly. Spiritual sound is the cornerstone of soul travel. It is a supreme deity projecting itself to all planes in all universes. Our soul catches these sound waves automatically and begins to travel according to our spiritual progress. The Master can take the Seeker to the designed experience. This happens when he wants to show you the experience differently. Divine light and sound are two pillars of God.

Everything is created through and by light and sound. Everything living, moving, flying or still has its being in light and sound. Light and sound are also our yardsticks while travelling. All these planes have different colours and sounds. Sometimes a little hint is given by the Master in the form of colour and sound, indicating where we have been. The total of light and sound become Spirit and Spirit is everywhere. So, you are always on the holy grounds upon which to meditate.

**Chakras:** There are about ten chakras in the body. The majority of practitioners deal with six or seven chakras only. They are spiritual centres or openings in the body; if we focus on one of them, we can contact the Spirit. At the time of death, the soul uses one of these openings to leave the body. All these chakras are physical organs that keep the body healthy; simultaneously, they are spiritual centres.

Some meditation groups specialise in specific chakras. Only a few possess the knowledge for all of them and know how to use them. If someone knows how to use the pituitary gland, pineal gland and Crown-Chakra, this individual will not bother with the lower chakras.

Lower chakras are used to gain psychic powers as they are attractive. These powers include making rain come or disappear, magic, materialising money. It is better to have a basic knowledge of these chakras. There is a brief explanation in our book Oh, My God if you wish to read it.

**Spiritual Master:** The spiritual Master is on top of the list. Without the Master, nothing is possible. You must have a Master before you join any spiritual path. He connects you with the light and sound and prepares all the paths so you can travel. He takes you through unknown tunnels when making inner journeys and introduces you to the lords and rulers of each plane and the guardians of the Golden Books.

He brings you back safe and sound and protects your physical body, resting somewhere in your house. He is responsible for ensuring that you remember your experience. Sometimes, he just gives you a little nudge, what you have seen because it could be a bit too much for you to digest. Experience is for the soul; that is what matters. This is just a brief description of the man who runs the show.

# THE MASTER TECHNIQUE

**Soul travel:** This is the main subject and we need to learn all the secrets to having success. Soul travel is merely a change of consciousness from one point to another. So, if you can shift your attention from one place to another, that is soul travel. It is your success but people will notice the change in your persona. Having dreams is also soul travel. Daydreaming is also soul travel. So, every person in the universes of God is doing soul travel in one way or another.

We are very successful at soul travel when we have big problems because we focus on the situation. This is more or less mental travel. We live the whole situation. We smell, touch, feel and breathe that situation. Even if someone asks us to come out of our travelling, we come out but we are back to square one after a while. The only snag is that we don't appreciate this type of travelling. Today, we will learn controlled soul travel; Your action and how you apply it to materialise the results.

The main aim is to master the technique and become the Master of your universe. Coming back to the chakras, some yoga groups use all the chakras. Maybe that is the way they know and have been taught. I sometimes wonder, if someone begins from the lowest chakra and progresses from there upwards, 'How long will it take to come to the point of the third-eye? This method looks pretty passive since we can begin from the spiritual eye and progress from there onwards.

**Pituitary gland:** It is between the eyebrows or base of the nose but two inches away from the forehead screen. It is the seat of the mind. It is a tiny bean-shaped body.

**Crown-Chakra:** This is the easy exit point for the soul to travel and at this point, Spirit enters the physical body and flows into the spine and reaches all chakras. This is why a straight posture, with the spine erect and the chin slightly up, is essential. Otherwise, the flow of the Spirit to the chakras will not be as good and resulting in unsuccessful experiences.

**Third-Eye (pineal gland):** This is the seat of the soul. This is where we focus our attention. We feel the soul's presence in the third-eye and the action required to exit it through the soft spot. In figure 1, all spiritual opening points are shown, although all the images are self-explanatory.

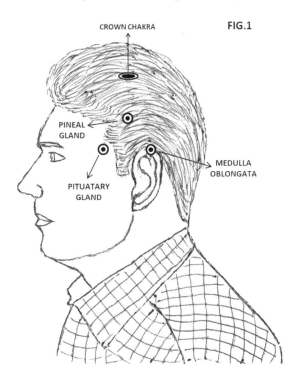

The third-eye is a gift from God so that the soul can see anything at any time. Two eyes are for physical use, as we are seeing now. The third-eye was used to have a spiritual experience at any time, such as communicating with the inner self. When attention was focused on the physical to the third-eye, people could see any place they liked. When aura changed to a being-ness state; the experience was live as we viewed images on a cinema screen.

The screen and projector are similar to the third eye in the cinema. The screen is where we put our attention. The projector is the focus reaching from the third-eye to the screen. As the yugas changed, we lost our spiritual gift or faculty faded into the background. We can have the same experience but we have to make some effort. People have forgotten their natural ability; who they were or their capabilities.

The majority of people today don't want to know anyway. Only a few Seekers are interested in learning who they are and what they can experience. This is why the term 'chosen ones' is used. There are not many people who can teach soul travel. Some claim they can; when you approach the experience, their claims disappear into nothing.

If you find the right Master who can help, it comes down to your effort. It has been said before when the Seeker is ready, the Master appears. This is the direct path to the Godhead and our approach is direct. Straight and narrow is the way. As Jesus said, 'Only a few will find it.' This is so true but still, some people know all the facts but are not successful.

In my opinion, they are not concentrating on the spiritual points or are not spending enough time. During the attention and the chanting of the holy word, the vibrations are stirred to experience. This is the place where you can have subjective and objective experiences. Either you can go within yourself or travel outwardly. It is just a matter of putting attention in different places.

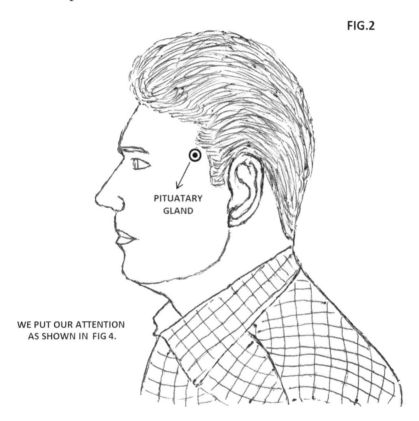

FIG.2

PITUATARY
GLAND

WE PUT OUR ATTENTION
AS SHOWN IN FIG 4.

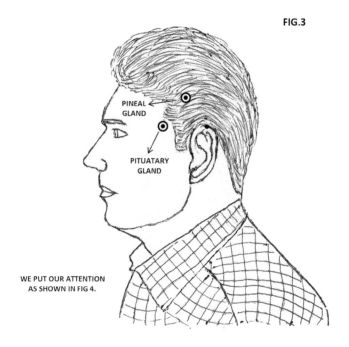

FIG.3

PINEAL GLAND

PITUATARY GLAND

WE PUT OUR ATTENTION
AS SHOWN IN FIG 4.

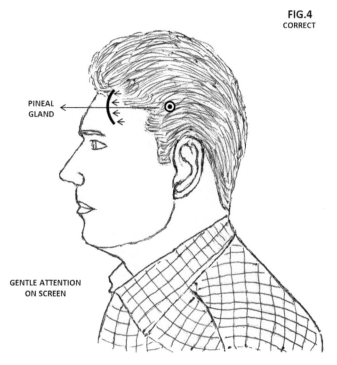

FIG.4
CORRECT

PINEAL
GLAND

GENTLE ATTENTION
ON SCREEN

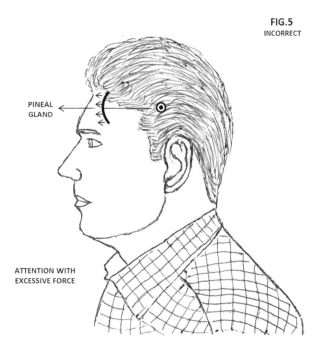

**FIG.5**
INCORRECT

PINEAL
GLAND

ATTENTION WITH
EXCESSIVE FORCE

**Figure 4:** Is the correct position to focus your attention. It is attention minus effort. An excessive effort will penetrate through the screen and the experience will be lost, as in **figure 5:** The screen is so near that focus must be very gentle and more or less in a 'pulling-back' position. It is even better if you don't look directly at the screen. Look at it obliquely. This improves the chance of having experiences.

**First approach:** You can chant your word and have the Master's picture on the screen. If he appears, he can do many things.

He can come and appear on the screen.
He can show you the light in many colours.
He can take you on an inner journey.
He can open up Akashic records or take you out of your body.

**Second approach:** Is for those Seekers who want to have out-of-body experiences. This time, you can change the position of your attention from the screen to the experiencer, which is the soul itself. Gently push upward and through the soft spot on the top of the skull.

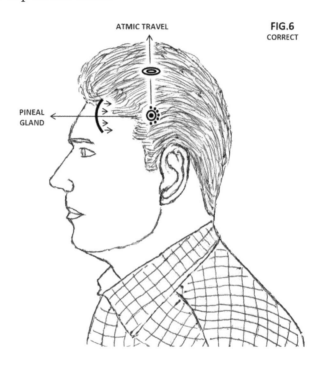

This time, we will forget the screen and not imagine anything. We will direct our attention or feelings to every imagination or feeling creator. It is sitting there and watching everything very gently. That is the soul Itself. (This is expressed as the black dots in **figure 6.**) This time, in that gentleness, you feel the soul's presence. Once you have established the presence, you have to circle your feelings around the soul.

Now, **gently try to lift yourself as soul** and it will come out through the soft spot on the top of your head. Once the soul becomes aware of itself, it has the natural ability to travel. If you encounter any difficulty, put your attention outside yourself, for example; on some solid object while trying to get out. As we discussed earlier, attitude and attention play an essential part in success.

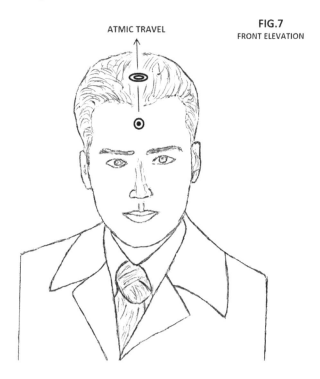

you have managed to pull yourself out of your body, try to stay in the room. Don't venture too far because the first few times, you will feel the pull of the silver cord. If you go too far, you will experience pain in your abdomen once you come back. This is nothing too serious. After a few times, you will get used to it. Once you have managed to get out; practice regularly. Otherwise, you may lose your skill, like any other. Practice makes perfect.

Now, I want you to practice and see how successful you are. You know what soul travel is and where the spiritual points are. How to shift your attention and how to pull yourself out. Once you know all this and become the master of this technique, all you have to do is sit down and chant your spiritual word a few times and you are out and everywhere.

Out-of-body travelling is limited to the subconscious plane. If you learn to shift your attention within the 'screen,' you can experience the higher planes with attention minus effort. First, we were travelling but now we are entering the zone of being-ness. We can further discuss soul travel in many other ways, such as through the medulla oblongata, dream travelling and direct projection (shifting yourself with your physical body).

May success be yours.

# SELF-REALISATION

Self-realisation is a widespread word used by almost all religions. This word carries a lot of weight. It has a unique pull for spiritual Seekers. They are willing to pay any price to the spiritual guru provided he can teach this knowledge and transport the Seeker into the soul plane. People are spiritually hungry and are desperate to achieve this realisation.

Self-realisation is not something someone can give you overnight, in a month or year. There is no guarantee as far as time is concerned. It depends on the Seeker's spiritual readiness to receive this experience and the ability of the teacher to provide this knowledge. It is less to do with knowing and more to do with spiritual awareness. If the student is ready, it is worth the struggle for the teacher; otherwise, it is a waste of time for both.

People do come for this realisation but it is found with experience. They are more or less only interested in solving their problems. With their limited knowledge, they think they will find peace after working out specific issues but that is the external approach. I wish peace were an external affair and readily available to everyone. If this were the case, it would probably go on sale.

Peace, awareness, unfoldment, realisation or whatever term you wish to call them, are subjective concepts and related to the inner. You need to learn how to go within yourself. The process is lengthy. It could take a short time or become a lifetime achievement. It can be achieved in a few months if the Seeker is sincere, disciplined and willing to follow the instructions from the Master.

It also depends on how unfolded you are spiritually. Your spiritual unfoldment shows that you have created good karma in the past. You will easily pick up the instructions and not panic during subjective travels if you have the background. When the Master leads the way, it is in the dream state or during your meditation practice. 'How willing are you to give up your negative habits? Most people fail because they want to achieve everything but do not want to sacrifice anything.

The Master does not ask for something which cannot be given up easily. The Master is not asking for anything to be given up at all. He is more interested in balancing the things and situations we encounter each day. He is aware of what you already know and as such, he will build up from there onwards. Every experience or step you take is a positive point. There is no going back. In the early days, the Master would work on the physical side of the knowledge through oral teachings.

This would establish a yardstick to compare your subjective travels through dreams, spiritual exercises or quick naps, which I find very effective. The experiences received through quick naps are short and to the point and you hardly lose any of their content. The early travels accommodate what you can handle as a truth. Excessive experience can put you out of balance.

There are a few spiritual cities in this world and some of them have spiritual 'Golden Books.' When travelling under the teacher's umbrella, the student is taken nightly to one of these cities, where the truth is revealed. Step by step, we proceed up to the astral plane to explore the new horizons and meet with the keepers of these books. These keepers are also responsible for holding the Satsang for the new apprentices, giving them extra tips individually.

Now, your spiritual knowledge is building up tremendously. As you progress, the sacred word given by the Master will also change and raise your vibrations to the next level. On these planes, you make many friends during regular visits. You may also make a few enemies as you are subjected to the lower worlds. Often, the entities, who don't like visitors, try to trap you or create illusory scenes to mislead you, the same as many people do in this world.

This is where the protection of the Master comes in handy. The astral plane is better than the physical plane but it is illusory. Your next way station will be in the seed world, also known by many other names, including the causal plane. The overall view is orange colour. It is why many Indian saints prefer to wear this colour. By doing so, they feel holy internally. This is the seed world or the memory house of past physical records.

You will hear the sound of tinkling bells. This plane is deeply connected with the Christian world, as the bells are the symbols in both churches and Hindu temples. In Hindu temples, all devotees must touch them as they proceed to pay respects to their deities. This shows how saints from all walks of life made their journey to this plane. Again, the teachings will be given in the Golden Temple in the presence of past Masters from Earth.

Attainment of knowledge from this world will lead you to the next. It requires sheer hard work and dedication of your time to control your internal and external affairs. All your efforts, along with the instructions of the Master, will lead you to the mental plane. All the aspects mentioned in the previous plane will change. This time, the tasks will be much more challenging and more torturous. During the; Dark Night of the Soul.

It will take longer to pass through this plane and you will struggle to control your mind and work on its weaknesses to balance them out. This process is necessary before any success to materialise on the mental plane. There are many attachments here that are not willing to leave. You cannot become a holy man based on your conditions. You have to obey the will of God to enter into the soul plane. After all the mental struggle; the wisdom you have received, the lord of that plane will show you the way.

This is a courtesy, as the Master knows all the secret tunnels. You have entered the soul plane and become aware of yourself as a soul. Now you come to know yourself; who you are. Before, you only knew yourself as 'I,' now you know 'I am.' This awareness of yourself as a soul is called Self-realisation. 'The next stage will be to understand what a soul is? This is just the beginning of a new phase in your life and the flow of spiritual learning has begun.

You were the traveller before but now you have entered into the world of being. The challenging task lies ahead; working towards God-realisation. This is not a full explanation of the higher worlds, merely a hint. To give a full explanation could take volumes of literature. After this realisation, you are still subject to the lower worlds. You must ensure you do not do anything wrong, which will bring your consciousness back down to the lower level.

The king of the hill either stays up or easily falls. Stay alert all the time and prepare yourself for the next step, which will be more exciting and blissful.

Now you know who you are.

# SATNAM JI

Satnam Ji is the first personification of God, which can be seen and talked to by any soul traveller. Upon meeting with this great super-being, you can say, 'Waheguru,' meaning, 'You are the greatest guru.' Those who have not met this spiritual giant are only in the field of imagination. I have met thousands of people in my walk of life. If you ask them, 'What does Satnam mean?

They will simplify it by following the alphabetic letters and splitting the name in half. 'Sat' means 'true' and 'nam' means 'word'; therefore, it means 'true word' or 'true nam.' The meaning is almost the same but it is one word. Guru Nanak was the only person who made this world aware of this spiritual giant, only after God. We are going to discuss this in the following paragraphs.

Guru Nanak was a regular visitor to Satnam and his residence is known as Sach Khand in Soul plane. I mention 'his residence' as we will also discuss this. Upon visits by Guru Nanak to this great Satnam, the only praise he could give was 'Satnam Waheguru.' 'Satnam' is the name and 'Waheguru' is his praise indicating there is no other guru who can supersede the personification of God.

On the first page of the Sri Guru Granth Sahib, Guru Nanak mentions his experience and shares, step by step, what he learned about God. He says Ikkonkar, meaning one and only universal creative God, who no one supersedes. This is why Ikkonkar is the first word. Satnam appears as the second word. If anyone is in charge after God, it is Satnam. This is why he is Waheguru, meaning most excellent guru.

**Karta-Purukh:** Karta means 'fully in charge of all Universes.' 'Purukh' (man) indicates his appearance in the male form. The following are the qualities he possesses.

**Nirbhau:** without fear. "As he dwells in the worlds of being."

**Nirvair:** without hatred. "Soul plane is pure Spirit."

**Akalmurt:** a personification of God. (Replica)

**Ajuni Se Bhang:** a person beyond birth and death. The re-incarnation system does not apply to Soul Plane.

**Gur Parsad:** by God's grace.

At the end of this spiritual verse, the Four Truths are mentioned.

**The three truths:** 'Omnipotent, Omniscient and Omnipresent' are accepted or mentioned by most religions. 'Nanak hossi bhee sach.' Guru Nanak could have written volumes of books on each word if he wished but his experience with God and Satnam Ji was so great that he followed the shortest route to explaining it. He left an open explanation to religious scholars to learn further.

If we follow the scripture step by step, we can draw a complete picture of this spiritual giant from two central angles, God itself and the lower worlds. The person who can understand the last two paragraphs with any success is spiritual in his own right in this world.

We are going to begin from this physical world, looking at the name of Satnam, how it comes into form. There are three grand divisions of God. The first is the lower worlds, which deal with the matter, energy, space and time. They are concerned with all material things, such as birth, death, karma, hell and heaven; anything that makes you happy or suffers is part of the lower world.

The second grand division is of pure Spirit. This is beyond the creation of karma. All souls do their allocated duties and live in a state of bliss. These are the worlds of being and there are no things that stand in opposition to each other, such as male and female, day and night, love and hate, birth and death. Now you know why Guru Nanak gave these expressions about Satnam Ji, such as Nirbhau, Nirvair, Ajuni se bhang.

Satnam Ji is established in soul planes by God to run the entire system. The soul can progress from the physical to the second grand division in this lifetime and most souls will remain in this second grand division for millions of years; it does not matter how unfolded they are. The second grand division is between the soul plane to Anami-Lok. After that, the third grand division begins.

This third grand division is out of reach, beyond description and allocated to the very few privileged souls who are either present or past Masters and to God itself. We follow the directions to Satnam Ji's name and where he rules well. On this physical plane, the ruler or the person in charge overall is called Elohim or Space God. He ensures the smooth running of this world.

The second is sukhsham desh or astral plane; the lord of this plane is Jot Niranjan. Here also resides Dharam-Raj, the person responsible for dead people and disciplining them according to their good or bad karma. The result is heaven or hell and back to the earth again to take new birth. This puts the soul back on track to unfold to its maximum.

The third step is the causal plane or karan-des, also known as the universe of memories because all records of our lives on the earth plane are stored here. The ruler is Omkar. This is the universe in which people engaged in looking at Akashic reading. You must be able to do soul travel; otherwise, this plane is out of reach.

The fourth is the mental plane, the world of Brahm. He is the ruler of this universe and controls all the universes below, right down to Earth. This is from where the three spiritual currents flow; Brahma, who creates; Vishnu, who preserves; and Shiva, who destroys. This is why Shiva is established on this planet Earth.

Next is the subconscious plane and the ruler here is Par-Braham. The tunnel to reach this plane is called Rukmani and the melodic sound is that of buzzing bees. The person who makes up this consciousness is called Nibbuta, which means 'next to a saint.' To reach the soul plane, one must go through Bhanwar-Gupha and the tunnel is called Yureka.

The fifth plane is called Sach khand or soul plane and the ruler or lord of this plane is Satnam Ji. This is the first world of pure Spirit and the threshold to the lower worlds. This is beyond day and night, birth and death. This is also the threshold from the lower worlds into the pure Spirit worlds. So, in the sense of speaking, this is the centre point from either side. God has no form, as we all know, so God has created Satnam Ji to represent itself to the eligible souls, those who wish to see God. So, this is the closest we can be in the presence of God.

Satnam Ji is personified Spirit (or word / Shabda) in the male form. It is a pure soul body but represents itself in the male form to give darshan (a glimpse) to the privileged souls who make it this far after their travels and succeed in a being-ness state. All the rulers **above** the soul plane communicate but are **hardly visible** even to soul bodies. Their soul bodies turn into mini-stars at the point of visits.

As you go higher, the stars even vanish but you can communicate and know the presence of each other. This will carry on up to the top of the second grand division. In the third grand division, communication is non-existent; these are the worlds (or planes) of total knowingness. As an ordinary soul cannot venture this far, God has created this great soul for us to see and communicate with.

Upon experiencing this great soul and its responsibilities and being directly responsible to God, Guru Nanak could not help saying 'Satnam Waheguru.' God is on top, expressed as Ikkonkar, as second to God. It appears as the second word, 'Satnam'. The words that follow are an explanation of Satnam and its position. Guru Nanak made the explanation very short and to the point.

Nowadays, all the scholars (gianis) turn these simple words into books. Sri Guru Nanak would have done this himself if this had been necessary. As these people don't have insight into the inner worlds, they perform all kinds of mental gymnastics. God would not be that far away if they put their effort into the inner search. Experience is as close as your heartbeat.

Satnam Ji runs all the worlds and universes, not only the lower worlds. He is also responsible above the soul plane. All worlds below were created according to the instructions of this great soul. All rulers, such as Par Brahm, Brahm, Omkar, Jot Niranjan and Elohim, were appointed by Satnam Ji.

Some religions claim that this world is created in six days and that God rested on the seventh day, which is called Sunday. 'I am wondering, what was the rush? God is not subject to anything such as time, yet each religion expresses this. Then they also contradict themselves by putting these conditions. It can create or destroy anything in a micro-spirit second.

Some people contradict other rulers, such as Brahm and Kal Niranjan and make remarks like 'Brahm is a clever and selfish God.' People who make such remarks have read this somewhere and taken the information as the word of the Bible, expressing this to others and showing how knowledgeable they are. These are people with book knowledge and no insight into the inner worlds.

Although these great souls are doing duties in the lower worlds, this does not mean they hold a state of consciousness according to that particular plane. These are highly unfolded souls and close to the supreme God. These souls are very near and dear to it. They are only doing their allotted duties as assistants. When we talk about the assistants of God, these are the souls we are talking about.

Every Seeker is striving to be an assistant with God. You never know; you might end up on the astral plane to deceive the new arrivals. Guru Nanak praised the great Brahm,

Par-Brahm and Sohang. These are the souls responsible for closing the floodgates, preventing souls from entering the soul plane. They keep you busy in your normal material chains and provide you with the shackles of the five passions.

Any saint at present who is interested in gathering money, making millions by investing in property or collecting donations, is not spared by Brahm. By following these types of individuals, you cannot go very far, as they are caught in the net of maya themselves. Being on soul plane, Satnam Ji is responsible for the well-being of all souls; Similarly, Brahm, Vishnu and Shiva are the creator, preserver and destroyer on the material side.

Any soul who manages to free itself from the lower worlds has its records removed from the causal to the soul plane and kept under the supervision of Satnam. As the soul progresses beyond the soul plane, its records will also be on the soul plane. There are different sections of the soul plane and records are in the relevant sections according to the level of unfoldment.

Most historical Masters and those who will serve in the future records are kept directly under the attention of Satnam Ji. Sincerely I wish to dedicate these few paragraphs to Sri Guru Nanak to contribute spiritual knowledge to this world. Now we see that Satnam Ji is the Karta-Purukh, the main player in the whole creation of God, Satnam Waheguru.

Later, during his spiritual sermons, Baba Nand Singh ji of Nanak Sar would mention his close relationship with Satnam Ji. His explanation was similar to the one I gave in this chapter. Those soul travellers into the spiritual planes can understand what has been said. Others can only imagine what has been said and draw their conclusions.

You cannot crack the clay pot into two pieces and then try to fill it with water. Similarly, you cannot split, the word **Satnam** into two and explain what it means.

# SPIRITUAL WISDOM

Spiritual wisdom is a gift from God. Some people are wise, well-read and mature in their circle. They can talk on any subject and advise on any matter and people trust them. They operate on a world level. Some of them may even be achievers of spiritual wisdom. People with spiritual wisdom are the right-hand assistants of God. God directs their lives. They live and have their being in Spirit and are more spiritual than physical.

Receiving wisdom is a continuous process. It can happen most of the day and continue while sleeping. The soul receives the messages and conveys them to the mind upon awakening and to be remembered. Wisdom may appear in one word or many words, which are easy to capture. It is never in lengthy dialogues which you cannot remember. The words may seem like a wave or they may drop like pearls.

It can appear in a written form or be listened. This entire process occurs within one area of the skull, the inner. 'It is all pure and neat.' I am not talking about when you are walking on the streets and you see something written on walls or someone whispers a word to you physically. The wisdom I am talking about is spiritual and it comes to you directly in a pure form. All you have to do is grasp the pearls of wisdom as they come to you.

First, capture them spiritually, process them mentally and then express them physically. Usually, insight is given to the people who can capture it, which does not disappear quickly. Capture it when it comes or writes it down before you lose it. This is precisely how holy books are written. Perhaps you have read a holy book and asked, 'How is it possible for someone to write like this? Well, they haven't.

The saint has received a direct message from God and managed to write it down on a piece of paper and present it to the world. I could have written quite a few books by now only if I had put the words I had received into written form. Nevertheless, it always comes back if you tune into the Spirit but it will never be the same as it originally appeared.

I am not a writer but I am stunned at such messages when they appear. The messages come from God to the soul and appear on the mental screen and then are passed over to the astral and expressed on the physical. Throughout this process, they may be in a diluted form. This is why they appear so clear in written form, on the screen or whispered so clearly. You cannot miss it. If you do not write immediately and try to remember it for later, I can assure you that you will lose 50 percent of it in no time.

When a message is received, your mind is almost blank as the Spirit creates the blank situation to pass on the message. The saints are in tune with the Spirit and are keeping their minds empty to communicate with the Spirit. This is how they get the answers to their followers' problems. They often say, 'I, of myself, do nothing. It is the Spirit that does the job.' This is true; they only act as God's channel or right-hand men.

Here we are not talking about left or right-handed magicians or psychic people who act as channels to ghosts or the negative force. These are pure messages from Spirit, a neutral force that is neither negative or positive. You can blank your mind if you wish but you cannot make the wisdom appear. It is the will of God. Wisdom can come day or night; mainly, it occurs during waking hours.

When it comes at night, you must wake up in a split second and write it down or you will lose most of it by the morning and sometimes it is lost completely. Wisdom is the dialogue between God and the receiver. Saints are the receivers of wisdom, making them different from normal people. They always dwell in spiritual worlds while we deal with physical or mental problems.

Wisdom is endless; there is no limit to it. Wisdom is pure love from Spirit to the individual recipient. The power of wisdom could save the world. After following the teachings for a year, the channel opened itself. There was a lot of sincere effort on my side and the guidance of the Master; otherwise, I would be no different from anyone else.

We are all the same and have the right to be in this world and beyond. Your past good karma brings you to the point where you are today. When wisdom appears, it is in no way a scanning of information. It is the direct message and the spiritual creativity working within. This is the true *dhyana* or **meditation**. The receiver always lives in the state of 'thy will be done' consciousness.

'If Spirit directs your life, what more could you want? You do not see God or become God but you directly connect with God. This is only available to a few fortunate ones but it is available for anyone to have, provided you find the right path and the Master to lead you to it. Spirit is a way of life, a means of living and enjoying your being-ness. Today is the day; tomorrow you may not find it.

May the Spirit be with you.

# SPIRITUAL HEALINGS

At least once in a lifetime, we all need spiritual healing. This could be for many reasons, such as physical disabilities or damage to the psychic bodies. Physical disabilities are many; broken bones, blindness, inability to walk, hearing problems, constant pain and diseases for which we have no cure. Most ailments can be cured with our present-day medicine but a few persist, seeming as if they will never leave us.

Medicine provides excellent remedies for our physical body. If the physical body has not responded to the treatment, the pain may come from deeper within. This is beyond the physical, where spiritual healing comes in. Spiritual healing can be applied to any physical ailment and be successful. These ailments include cancer and aids, where our present-day medicine has not been very successful.

In extreme cases, spiritual healing can work if the person giving the healing is honest about his ability to do it. Many just pretend. Many pains come from deep within but the physical body only acts to express its existence. Throughout this book, I have mentioned our psychic bodies and they may have received damage somehow. The reasons are far too many to discuss; we will discuss these inner damages or pains to a minimum.

You need spiritual healing with this kind of pain, as present-day medicine may not respond. The heart, pituitary gland, pineal gland and medulla oblongata are spiritual centres and parts of our body, so the medication works. There are many types of spiritual healers in this world. They belong to many respected religions and they have their way of providing spiritual healing. Sufi saints are very famous and Christians have their own. Many of their branches offer this service.

Many cults and black magicians are trying to do the same. The success of the healing depends on the ability of the healer. I witness the healer providing this service and the approach is as follows; The person in suffering must visit the healer. This healer sits in silence and touches the affected body area with his hands, gently moving them forward and backwards while reciting spiritual words silently. The person concerned must pay a few visits before any real success materialises.

It is an astral approach and it does work up to some extent. There are also oracles throughout this world and many are still alive on a spiritual basis. Upon visiting them, the pain vanishes. Dargah Sharif of the old Sufi saints is very famous. A few places of Kali Mata of Hinduism are also famous and a few places of Sikhism do the same. It does not matter how famous or spiritual these places are. None of them will work unless the person concerned does not doubt in his mind when visiting them.

You must have a single-minded, positive approach; the healing is assured. Any doubts will make holes in your aura of process. Many healers provide healing over the phone and in return, they ask for a fee. Some healers provide permanent healings, while many will keep you hanging on, as they do not want to lose you as their customer. Healing is a gift from God and it should be provided free of charge or for donations freely offered.

The healer can lose the power of healing by misusing the spiritual gift from God. Once the power is lost, it will appear as if they are doing the job but there will be no significant results. The healer has to live and act his life on a purely spiritual basis. This is why not everyone is a healer, while sufferers are many. The true spiritual Master can heal his followers with or without any communication if it is required. The Master always knows the suffering of his followers.

You can send a request in writing or in silent communication; it will not make any difference. The healing is given unless the Master has purposely created the suffering for his student to ensure spiritual advancement. The Master will sit and watch the tolerance of his follower until the purpose is served. Once it is over, the follower will feel joy and peace within. I have witnessed the healing provided by my Master on my body.

While training one day, I injured some parts of my body by overexerting myself. I was in a lot of pain but I did not request the healing. The Master appeared in his soul body at midnight, even though he was in America physically. He woke me up and applied the pure spiritual vibrations to the affected area of my physical body. It was a joy to receive them. They were very warm and such a magnificent flow of vibrations surged through my body, giving me such a pleasant feeling that it was beyond description.

It lasted no more than two to three minutes and then he asked me to continue with my remaining sleep pattern. When I woke up in the morning, the pain was gone and it had never returned to the same area. It is not that difficult for those interested in learning how to do it. You must do this for free and in the name of God. The person concerned will approach you with a long-term illness or pain in a particular part of their body.

Under no circumstances must you touch the person as this will divert the karma into your physical body. Let the Spirit be in control. As you face the patient, sit in silence and chant your spiritual word silently. This will clear any wandering thoughts you may have and raise your vibrations. Prepare yourself and concentrate on the affected part of the body or the ailment in question.

At first, the approach will be mental and with total devotion to the Spirit, it will raise your vibrations to the soul itself. Upon success, release these vibrations to the affected area for two to three minutes and then quit by saying, 'May the blessings be.' If you are working on the whole body, it can take longer. Success depends on the vibrations raised at that time. You can close your eyes if it makes you feel more comfortable. It is the Spirit doing the job; we are only its channels.

# TO GOD, NO COMPETITION

People do not realise that there is no competition on the way to God. There is competition in every single field in this world. The areas are many; politics, sports, education, science, theatre and business. I have never seen any competition between saints, as there is none. They will offer compliments if they know someone is doing better. If any person or organisation tries to stop you from performing this good cause, they are not serious God-believers. More likely, they are merely business-minded people.

Only one power will try to stop you; the Kal or negative power. It will make every effort to stop and mislead you. We should be thankful to Kal because it brings sufferings to us. These are blessings in disguise, as our creator God is trying to polish us, similar to how a goldsmith polishes his jewellery. Without the participation of Kal, it would not be possible. God is the creator of the soul and Kal is the spinner of its journey. As Kal becomes the cause and in return, we become the effect, karma is created in our account.

The Kal is the first cause; the person who becomes the cause for you is the second cause and in return, you become the effect. The saints do not compete with anyone but there is competition within to get out of this world. I have been doing my spiritual endeavour in my own time and private house. According to my diary, I have managed eight times to be in the presence of God so far. As we all know, God is alone and we have the quality of being individual, so it is an entirely personal approach.

There is nothing to buy and sell but many disappointments, as success comes only after many failures. I don't know why people do not bother to enter this field. In this field, there are no boundaries and as they say, 'The sky is the limit.' The sky is just around the corner; even a split second will be too long. It is up to you. Those who think you cannot do it have an attitude of failure. Do not listen to anyone. It is your private affair. If people believe in what you know, that is good.

'If they don't, do you care? The answer is no, as you are not doing it for name or fame or anyone else; it will be your achievement. It is a personal journey, as education is essential to make your way in this world. Once you have achieved it, the knowledge will stay with you for the rest of your life. No one can take it away from you. In the same way, spiritual knowingness is also your achievement. Once it is in your grasp, no one can take it away from you.

Nor can you share it with many, as they do not hold the same state of consciousness. People love to argue with their little mental knowledge and they will try to bring you down to their level. It will be more or less a mental hash bash. I suggest you leave them alone. One day, they will know too. I love to encourage everyone to do the same, as this is the only worthwhile effort in your life. It should be your ultimate goal, as all other measures are a waste of time.

God is yours to have and it is waiting for you.

# CELEBRITIES

The saints are not celebrities. They are the messengers of God and are doing, what they have been directed to do. They are not interested in becoming celebrities. I have a reason for writing on this topic. I heard that a known spiritual person wanted to achieve celebrity status a while back. I was shocked to learn this because celebrities are the property of the public.

Saints are the property of the one and only God. They do have followers but they are not anyone's property. Anyone can follow the Master sincerely, who guides and helps the followers on a spiritual basis. The saint is responsible for all and at the same time, he is detached. It does not matter who is following or not; he does not look back. His sole purpose is to help those souls who are ready. The true spiritual Master always stays away from the limelight.

He hides from the glamorous lifestyle as much as possible because he is a very simple person in nature and deeds. He lives a very simple life. Celebrities come and disappear into thin air in no time, never being heard of again. On the other hand, Saints are sent to this earth purposely by God, they are given birth and their names live on forever, such as Guru Nanak, Jesus Christ and Buddha, to name just a few. Saints are not interested in achieving any status as such.

However, God's power invested in them is far greater than we can imagine. The saints prefer to stay anonymous and do their job. If no one knows them, they feel much better. They are not interested in names or praises. To be known by God is the most important achievement. If it knows you, I will say everyone knows you, one way or the other. I wonder if the saints begin to do celebrities' jobs, 'What would the celebrities do?

We are here to guide and assist anyone who needs it to lead a good spiritual life.

# THE SADNESS OF THE MASTER

The sadness of the Master is due to various world situations. For example, some countries are so short of food that people are starving and due to many diseases, children die at a very early age. These situations fall under the category of group karma. The governments are running the show. Some are successful, many struggles and some are helpless. The Master can help spiritually and he uses some of his initiates in their soul bodies to give peace to the individuals crying out for God's help.

Being the representative of God on this planet, the Master helps as much as possible or he is allowed. Other activities in this world are far worse; criminal offences, murders, drug crimes, rape of very young children or the very elderly and those who are helpless. Looking at these situations, most people ask; 'Is there a God? 'Why doesn't it do something? 'Why doesn't the Master intervene?

This is the play of Maya (illusion). God is responsible for the creation but the duties are divided into the lower worlds. The spiritual Master does his job and the negative or Kal power does its job. The negative force creates these unpleasant situations. These situations will remain and with time, they will worsen, as we know the Kal is still very young. All this will carry on as long as we are in the lower worlds.

The Master cannot interfere because if he does, then the duty of Kal Niranjan vanishes and the whole purpose of schooling for the souls is lost. The Master says, 'I am here to gather up the souls who are ready spiritually and wish to leave this world.' The Master is aware of these negative situations but cannot intervene everywhere unless asked. The Master feels very sad, as he is also helpless. He cannot break the spiritual law known as psychic space.

There are millions of people who create heavy karmas and as a result, millions and billions of people suffer. Some suffer due to their doings in the past but those watching feel pity for them. There are also cases in which people are genuine and innocent but still suffer. That is sad indeed.

# INTERNET

The Internet is one of the most profound sources of information available today. The world is connected as a whole. Information on all the subjects is available at your fingertips. Businesses have become more effective and efficient. The ordering of goods and payments is dealt with via the laptop, at your convenience. Computers are the way forward. However, if improperly used, they can be dangerous.

Improper means; transmitting pornographic materials, especially to young children, which is condemned worldwide. These innocents should be left alone to develop at an average pace. Sensitive information about nuclear technology, explosives and terrorist tactics is also very dangerous. The world is scary enough as it is. Computer hacking is another problem. Gaining secret information or interfering in another country's security can have dreadful consequences.

There are thousands of other wrongful means. I am not a computer person myself. I do not know how to operate one entirely but I will learn as soon as possible, as I will need it. It has come to my attention that many religious-based contradictions are evident today. People accuse each other by saying this religious teacher or religion has stolen information from that religion. A spiritual guru in America (anonymous) has been accused of stealing religious information from Asian countries.

I am not here to defend anyone, as I am not getting anything from it. However, to put some people's minds at rest, I will say not all of it is true. Some religious information can be adopted from here or there and with a bit of twist in writing, later, you can claim it to be yours.

There is lots of information and places to be seen on the inner. These places have fixed names and upon visiting and coming back to this world, we have no authority to change them in writing or verbally. I am trying to point to the names of the higher planes and their respective rulers. These rulers above are so powerful and knowledgeable beyond our imagination.

If someone tries to tell you about them, you'll find it hard to accept because it is beyond your reach but these beings are scanning this and other universes simultaneously. Regular spiritual visitors to the higher planes cannot twist their names in speaking or writing. You will be answerable for these changes and you will have to pay for the consequences.

I will give you an example. I am Londoner and know that millions of foreigners come to visit London every year. At least 50 percent of them will see similar places and things in London. The famous places to see in London include the Houses of Parliament, Big Ben, River Thames, London Bridge, museums, Trafalgar Square, Piccadilly Circus, etc.

If hundreds of people from all walks of life see London Bridge, they will use the same name to describe it when they return to their respective countries. When they write in a diary or someone attempts to write a book about their holidays in London, the words will be very similar. For example, 'I went to see London Bridge on 1 July 2010' or

'I was standing in the middle of London Bridge on Monday and saw two boats on the river Thames.'

All these visitors to London Bridge will mention this name in their writings worldwide. It is the same story for spiritual travellers at the inner or above. They see or visit the same places and write down their experiences. When a third person reads the spiritual works of other religions, similarities will appear, as these travellers are talking about the same places. These places are beyond human reach, so they cannot be claimed by any religion or country.

They are universal and to be claimed by anyone who can make it that far in travelling or they are as close as your heartbeat on the inner. This is the riddle you must solve. Many people are aware that there is a universal treaty about the Moon. Anyone can land on the Moon but no one can claim its ownership.

The person who has taken the trouble to look into the works of this American guru and then compares them with particular Asian religious writing is indeed a religious person. Otherwise, this person would not have bothered to spend all this time researching and releasing the information on the Internet. If anyone can take my examples seriously, they can divert their energies to positive means. I am sure you can gain some spiritual grounds for yourself. With luck, you can even visit these places for yourself.

If you suspect someone of wrongdoing, leave it to the Spirit. In return, they will reap what they sow. We are in no position to point the finger at anyone. Some religions claim to be beyond religion on the Internet and in their writings. This is not true. The words 'beyond religion' are attractive to say, hear and believe. When you look deep into any religious writing, they all indulge in dos and don'ts or they try to appear better than the others.

Similarly, if a religion holds copyrights over certain words and dictates that others cannot use them, this is part of the dos and don'ts. While reading the last few lines, you may have noted you set certain limits for yourself and others. This is also an indication of dos and don'ts. You must realise that you are beyond nothing. You are no different from any other religion. All the religions in the lower worlds operate similarly, as they feel the threat from each other. Domination is on the agenda.

'Beyond religion' means total freedom, within and to others. I know of one power that I believe is beyond religion; that is God itself. God does not put any restrictions on any person or religion. You can believe in God or you can ignore it completely. It has provided you with free will. You can love it or hate it, as some do. In return, it does not complain or punish anyone in any manner. It sends its messengers to convey its message of love and good virtues.

In return, the people create a new religion in the name of its messengers. Several religions are fighting with each other. It never complains but watches in silence in its neutral way. Any person or religion that dares to adopt its qualities can indeed claim to be beyond religion.

Purposely, I have not read the Qur'an, Bhagavad Gita, Bible or the Guru Granth. This is only for one reason; I did not want my writings to be influenced by other religious writings. Once I publish this book, I may read them to gain general knowledge. No one should feel discouraged by reading someone else's opinion expressed on the Internet. Every person has the right to express their opinion and you have the right to accept or reject it.

Spirit is always with you.

# HEALTH

Spiritual education is not complete without a discussion on health. The physical body is known by many names, such as 'clay shell' or temporary housing for the soul. For this reason, it must be treated as a temple. Also, it is our physical identification to be known as a person in this world. 'How many people can see the soul or be aware of its presence? Not many.

We are physical, known by a particular name and a personality is developed around this individual. This individual has the task of survival in this world. It does not matter if the body is working under the influence of your mind or soul. Neither can survive or show their presence without the physical body. A healthy body is a must for the mind and soul and we carry out our daily chores for physical survival.

Many people are naturally gifted with fit and muscular bodies, while others are average and a few unfortunate ones are born disabled. No matter what shape we are in, we are responsible for keeping it healthy. The percentage of people who look after themselves is low. Most of them are too busy earning their living to make ends meet. While some are busy making money, some are mentally disturbed due to family problems and some are disabled.

We eat, work and sleep under all these circumstances, following the same routine for years. One day, we realise our youth has gone and our body has decayed. Wrinkles are everywhere, our skin and muscles have lost their vitality and we are on the verge of old age. Many people look far older than their actual age, while a few looks so young physically that they appear half their age.

This is the difference if you look after yourself. A few people are naturally blessed to look young. You are going against the clock. Every day, you are growing older and age will take its toll sooner or later. We all go through childhood, youth, middle age and old age. Now we know that we depend on this physical body during all our phases of life. It is our responsibility to maintain health all through the years.

Poor health can be responsible for many miseries, physical ailments and depression. You will notice that people do not like being around a sick or depressed person. If you are healthy, you look better, work better and people around you feel motivated. Your happiness and good health are reflected in your personality. There are many ways to look after your body. The food you eat should be healthy and provide all the nourishment required each day.

Fast food or what we call junk food, should be avoided. In the old days, we used to cook at home and we were fully aware of what we were eating. In these times, we also did more manual labour than we do today. Nowadays, most office-based jobs and fast-food chains are available on every high street. Food is ordered over the phone and delivered to your doorstep.

'When it is available this easily, who wants to cook? Everyone knows that junk food is tasty but not healthy. Drugs are the worst enemy of health. There are many types of drugs, far too many to mention. The use of dirty syringes and drugs in the body is deadly to passing the viruses, such as aids or others, from one person to another. These drugs are costly and maintaining this lifestyle requires money.

Any person on hard drugs cannot hold a steady job. To feed this habit, the person will go to any level of degradation. The majority of burglaries and robberies are carried out to satisfy their cravings. Due to this bad habit, one person can bring misery to many people, including their parents, the people they have robbed, stabbed and the police. Above all, they have ruined their health.

**Smoking**: This bad habit is responsible for injuring internal organs, destroying the lungs and causing cancer. The smell is the worst part for people around you.

**Alcohol**: It is dangerous when taken in excessive doses. Under the influence of alcohol, behaviour changes, manners loosen and fights to break out. Driving in this condition is dangerous to oneself and others. Many road accidents result in death or permanent injury. Under this influence, we make commitments that we forget by morning. I do not drink and do not recommend anyone do so. I used to drink in my younger years, so I understand that pattern of behaviour.

Many people drink to forget their problems, which leads to alcoholism. This is the cheapest way to entertain the self. Find the root of your problem and try to dissolve it as soon as possible using your creativity, provided by nature, instead of indulging in alcohol. Drinking is not the solution and never has been. There are so many drug-related habits that are bad for your health. We will not discuss them all, as the list is endless.

**Eating disorders**: Both overeating or not eating enough are unhealthy. Loose muscles in the midsection are the first sign of poor health. Some people eat just enough to survive, which is unhealthy; it leaves our muscles on the verge of starvation. This can lead to many ailments.

We should eat the required amount to maintain our natural build. Our body has the natural ability to draw all the vitamins, minerals and proteins we need, provided our diet is healthy. Most of the food we eat should be almost fat-free but we require some fat in the body.

**Artificial vitamins**: Synthetic vitamins and minerals should not be used very early age. The body may get used to these artificial means. Similarly, doctors do not recommend the excessive use of antibiotics. The body may get accustomed to this habit and lose its natural ability to fight against the disease.

**Wear and tear**: Excessive use of the body, working long hours but not eating enough or at regular intervals will wear and tear on one's physical health. It is often too late by the time we come to our senses. Many people suffer from heart attacks, strokes, high blood pressure, brain haemorrhages and paralysis.

**Total rebuild**: We must adopt a positive attitude and start a total-rebuild program whenever we realise this in life. Do this and you will be successful. I admire many people who are disabled but perform better than able people. If you watch the Paralympics, you will be surprised to see how they perform. These people have put their disability to one side and moved on to materialise their goals.

**Freshen up:** Every day is important to us but we waste half of it being lazy. I suggest you must discipline yourself. After freshening up, you must stretch your body for five minutes or perform light exercises every morning. This way, your body will stay active for most of the day.

**Walking:** Walking is an excellent daily exercise. Jogging, rope-skipping, press-ups and sit-ups all help build stamina for men and women. Likewise, many video workout programs are available for ladies to stay active or lose extra fat.

**Yoga:** Yoga exercises help tone up all muscle groups and build stamina. Breathing exercises eliminate many ailments, as lots of oxygen is drawn into the body. It also allows you to maintain a youthful look. People who perform these exercises regularly will stay healthy and hardly feel sick. Many long-term illnesses can be cured. I am not a yoga follower but I do regular workouts to stay active and fit in my private gym.

**Shapata dand:** A compound move consisting of a press-up followed by a sit-up, on continuous rotation, for a few minutes. This exercise is very similar to burpees. This exercise is excellent for professional sportspeople, as it helps to build strength and stamina.

**Bodybuilding:** An excellent overall training program, bodybuilding is mainly based on using free weights and various machines available in most gyms. Regular exercise and eating healthy foods will remain strong and fit if your body is built genuinely. Many people want to cut corners to achieve a muscular physique by using drugs. This is very dangerous.

Under the influence of anabolic steroids, the muscles respond to exercises and growth happens quickly. In a short time, the muscles grow like watermelons. They look good but when the drug is discontinued and practice has stopped, the muscles shrink back to normal size and sometimes they appear flabby. Excessive use of drugs damages our internal organs and leads to many ailments.

**Feel-good factor**: When all muscle groups are fully pumped, the individual feels better. However, during the off-season or when the exercise programs have stopped, some people get depressed. It is advisable to exercise as usual and eat healthy foods. These are some basic exercises that can be beneficial to building the body overall.

## Chest
1. bench press
2. incline and decline press
3. close-grip bench press/lateral dumbbell press

## Shoulders
1. standing front barbell press
2. barbell press behind neck, also known as military press
3. lateral (to the side) dumbbell raises
4. front dumbbell raises to at least shoulder level

## Arms (biceps and triceps)
Biceps
1. standing barbell curl
2. single dumbbell curl and preacher bench curls

Triceps
1. close-grip bench press or triceps extensions
2. pulley machine push-downs
3. standing triceps dumbbell or bar extensions

## Back
1.  bent-over rows
2.  chin-ups (palms facing you)
3.  pull-ups (palms facing out) or pulley machines

## Legs
1.  squats
2.  front squats
3.  hack squats
4.  leg curls and leg extensions
5.  deadlifts

## Calves
1.  Calf raises on the machine
2.  Standing position

## Abdominals
Lie on your back and raise your head and chest area to form abs in the midsection while exhaling air from the lungs. Front or side leg raises will build different parts of the abdominal muscle group.

Nowadays, there are excellent machines available to develop any individual body part. We all live once; I suggest you better live well. Happiness is a sign of good health. To have a smile on your face costs nothing. At the same time, internal happiness is very important. This is your life; make the most of it.

Good health to you.

# DEATH

Death is that truth that no one wants to face. It scares everyone except a few. Hearing the word 'death' brings a shivering sensation to your mind and body. It is a dramatic experience, especially when our loved ones lose their lives. You do not want to hear or believe this. If the person is not related to your family, it does not bother you as much because there is no physical attachment. This **'attachment'** makes all the difference.

If we learn the art of detachment, then nothing can dramatically affect our lives. Everyone born is bound to die one day; this is the truth. We all know it but we don't want to face it. There is a saying; When the cat hunts, the pigeon, being in danger of death, closes its eyes but that does not make the cat disappear. The cat is still there to hunt but the pigeon doesn't want to face the danger. We all are in the same boat.

There are ways of going through this experience with less pain and people have different beliefs. The well-known saint Kabir told us that he was dying daily through the routine of leaving the body at will and travelling to explore the other universes. He mastered leaving his body at will to dwell in the places where people go after death. He conquered the fear factor and was happy to learn where he was going after death. It is a better place than where you are living now.

That was his message to the people; Do not fear; you have nothing to lose. You will be happier. There are or were saints who solved this mystery of death. They are here now in this world but you have to look for them. Every spiritual person you come across is not a saint. The message of all these saints is the same; to be detached. This will make life easier and less painful.

In Sikhism, this journey of life is expressed as a dream. From birth till death, time goes so fast that it feels like a dream. The ending of this long dream is called 'death' as we understand it. This is a true awakening in the spiritual sense. People are afraid when they learn that they will die, leave this physical body forever and enter into the worlds of the unknown, expressed as heaven and hell. You might celebrate this occasion and say, 'Thank God I am getting away from here if you know the other side.'

People are very naïve; we go through this process every day, during sleep. It is almost a 'next to death' experience but in the back of our minds, we are confident that we will wake up. Don't forget; some do not wake up. This is known as passing away during sleep. Physical death means waking up from this long dream and walking into reality. There are varying beliefs about what happens to the physical and soul body at the last hour of life or death.

However, some religions agree on one principle; At physical death, the King of the Dead angels appear at the bedside. As the dying person finishes their last breath, the angels escort the soul to the place of the lord of karma. He passes the judgement according to your karma and where the new arrival should go to heaven or hell. The king of the dead is in the male form but expresses itself through the astral body as being on the astral plane.

Some religions agree on this process but they begin to contradict their own beliefs and teachings at death. For example, in England, the funeral takes place one week after death. Then, the same priest who performs the ceremony says that the dead person's soul wanders around until the body is cremated or buried. Some believe that the soul will stay around until the priest or pundit says specific prayers. If we go through all this, we will find hundreds of beliefs that contradict the teachings of one's religion.

I hope they make up their mind about what they believe in, religion or superstition. The physical body is to the person, as the nest is to the bird. Once they leave the place, they just forget about it and make a fresh start in their next life. The soul is always moving, beginning a new experience in a new body that is already prepared for it. The body and soul fit as a glove fits the hand; all the conditions are met for the new journey.

The conditions for the soul to leave the physical body are as soon as it becomes incapable of staying alive. Then the Soul has to leave it forever. The reasons are many; old age, terminal illness or accidental death. In the case of accidental death, the Soul may wander around for a while, as the accident happened outside the allotted time and the soul is in shock (physical expression) because the accident was not expected.

The angels were not waiting for the soul to be collected but later, the soul would find its way. If not, it can wander around until its allotted time is over. During that period, it can get caught in the traps of black magicians and misused for evil purposes. This is another phase of life. Not all accidental death cases turn into ghosts or wandering souls.

To give you peace of mind, I will provide you with an example.

Look at the animal kingdom. 'Do you know most of the animals in the jungle are hunted by other animals? Likewise, millions of chickens, cows and pigs are slaughtered daily to provide food. 'Did you realise all these are accidental deaths? According to this theory, all these animals should have turned into ghosts or wandering souls and this world would be full of them but we hear nothing of it. Souls do find their way back on their natural accord.

At the time of death, give your proper respects to your loved one. Do not follow any superstitions that will disrespect the body. The last ceremony should be as simple as possible, with complete sincerity; that is all it requires. Let go of the departing soul as soon as mentally possible because it has already left the body. It is easier said than done but as the saying goes, 'Time is a great healer.' God has given us the strength to do this. Oh My God, our book explains the final moments of death and your stay in heaven or hell.

Yes, in Oh My God, you may find the truth.

# THE RIDDLE OF GOD

The riddle of God is a highly complex subject for the human mind to grasp. We will look at it from the surface view, as no one can understand or explain; unless you are a spiritually awakened person and have had enormous experience in this world and the universes beyond. This is an in-depth study, as your soul and billions of others exist in the lower worlds. There is not much study you can do in the purely spiritual world, as the action is next to nothing.

The environment or atmosphere above is next to Godly in nature. The thoughts of the mind do not operate above, so there is no chance to analyse the subject and solve the riddle of God. There is a lot of action and reaction, suffering and joy, in the lower worlds. You wonder what the mystery of God might be. There is a universal body. It is the totality of everything or whatever you can imagine.

It includes this world, the stars, Moon, Sun, universes and the void you cannot even see. This world is minimal; all countries, land and water form into the shape of a ball or what we know as the globe. The universal body has no beginning or end. It has a shape or no shape and is beyond understanding, as it is infinite. It has chosen one place in the universal body to reside or throne, yet it is everywhere.

The human body is made similarly; the brain controls it physically and the soul in spiritual terms. The soul and brain have similarities and both reside in the head area yet control the whole body. Medical research declares that the body is useless when the brain is dead. When the soul leaves the body, it is said to be dead in spiritual terms. God is everywhere, also residing in one place, somewhere high. All of the creation, the void, space, fire, air, water, light and sound, everything we see externally, is also within us.

We can go within to get the experience or it has enabled us to travel externally. The mind is more satisfied with external travel because we are physical and this approach seems more natural. No one wants to close their eyes and look into the dark void for long hours. The mind has no patience. God has created the whole of creation and each atom is part of the universal body. Each physical form, which is in the process of growth with time, has a soul.

No matter what shape it is; man, woman, land animal or bird; God experiences itself through each form. This is known as the Wheel of Eighty-Four. The creation is finished but multiplication is in progress. All universes are created for the soul to have experience. 'What will be the shape of this large void? No one knows apart from God itself; The Soul or It is known as Paramatma, Allah.

'Param' means 'super' and 'Atma' means 'soul.' So, it is the 'Super Soul,' and it has created all souls and given them the qualities and abilities of 'The Soul.' Likewise, all souls are part of it. The Super Soul is one but its creation comprises billions, trillions and more. Each soul is individual and retains its individuality throughout its journey. It is a known factor in spiritual studies; it has created all these souls in its image, yet it has sent them down into the lower worlds for schooling.

Upon maturity, the soul will return to its true home as an assistant for God. God is so great and its knowledge is beyond our imagination. 'If God is beyond our knowing, why did it create all these souls, which are part of it and have all its qualities? 'Why has it sent them down to experience? **This is the riddle.** The souls make their journey downward into the lower worlds. The journey has begun; the mind, five passions and karma become part of the experience.

The soul is trapped under the veil of illusion and suffering has begun. It is physical suffering and mental torture, yet the soul resides in a neutral state to gain experience. The suffering, hardship and mental torment are beyond tolerance. To file our petitions, we seek peace from place to place; church, masjid and temple. When the pain is beyond our tolerance, we cry out to God, 'Please help me. Save me.' But there is no answer.

It does not intervene. If it does, then the whole purpose of schooling in the lower worlds is lost. The person who is suffering and desperate for the answer but unable to see or hear anything loses faith and declares that there is no God. Their suffering and instability in life are due to the bad karma created in these or previous lives. The creation of bad karma and its payments are discussed in the chapter, 'Karma.'

God as a whole is in all the atoms, millions and trillions of them, yet individually it suffers in all forms of life. The mental tortures of a million types; loss of limb, blindness, deafness, terminal illnesses, too many to name, are part of the learning process. Each soul experiences through the physical and other lower bodies and the mind create all the drama.

When we cry out for help and receive no answer, **the answer is within the answer**. If God wanted to solve each soul's problems so easily, it would not have sent them for education in the lower worlds. If it intervened to help any soul, the learning process would be disturbed. We do not realise that it is experiencing itself through each of us, as individual souls. It is educating every atom of the universal body. It can wipe the slate of your karma clean but this does not serve the original purpose.

It is believed that God provides food for all its creation, yet it goes hungry at night. If we realise that it is the creator and the sufferer, we should leave its process to proceed in its own accord. On the stage, it is the creator, the player and the sufferer. It is experiencing the whole process through each of us, all the time. **This is the riddle of God**. If we understand this, life becomes much easier. Otherwise, our sufferings are many.

Be prepared to tolerate or let God tolerate itself.

# THE WILL OF GOD

The will of God is the main factor of each life-form, as nothing can exist without it. We exist because God wills it. God itself is the life force behind everything in existence. All else are the attributes it uses to make a system run. It has a spiritual hierarchy in the higher spiritual worlds; The Spirit, the lords of the planes and the keepers of God's word in wisdom temples. A similar hierarchy exists in the lower worlds and the Master of the time, which gathers the souls to prepare them for the final journey.

'What is the will of God? All souls are here to experience and return to assist in the worlds of God. This is the primary purpose, as God is neither for or against anything. It exists everywhere. There is no land or space that does not share its qualities, from a root of grass to a man and worlds beyond. It encompasses the entirety of creation. That is free will. So, it lets the whole system run of its free will.

You and I have been given the full authority to run our lives as we wish but it has attached one of its attributes, called karma, to monitor the soul's progress. We can run our lives wisely or as wild animals and we will be held responsible accordingly. The soul is part of it but God feels no pain or pleasure due to its suffering, as it is neutral. Being neutral as its creator, the soul itself is not in a position to create karma, to roll the ball. The mind and the lower bodies are attached to it and the journey begins.

Soul itself hardly suffers. It is the mind that is the creator of all the wrongdoings via the channels of the lower bodies. When it comes to all our problems, accidents, loss of limbs, sickness, wealth and poverty; the physical body and other bodies suffer and torture the mind when situations are not to their liking. The soul only registers what has taken place and what it has gained as an experience. When we are unhappy or our minds are not satisfied, we cry out to God and say, 'God, why are you doing this to me? 'What have I done to deserve this?

Sometimes we pray and show our fists but there is no response either way because it has given the responsibility to the Lord of Karma. The Lord of Karma has one law; 'The Mill of God grinds slowly but it grinds exceedingly well. Whatever you sow, you will reap.' When all the prayers and petitions fail and your sufferings are beyond your control, you conclude and say, **'It must be the will of God.'**

It does not interfere when you are committing grave errors and it does not interfere either when you are suffering. It is beyond suffering. The soul itself has the same qualities. This is why your soul never dies. All else attached to it turns to ashes or dust. We complain because in this life, we cannot see any wrongdoing. People are unaware that our present life is based on our five to six previous lives.

No one likes to suffer but everything happens for good. It is your mental torture but it could be your soul's gain from experience. Usually, it lets the system run as it is but when people begin to create wrongdoings beyond tolerance, they disturb the system and the Lord of Karma takes action. The results are big disasters such as earthquakes and tsunamis. These happenings remind people who is in control.

Wherever these happenings occur, you will notice many harmful activities in that part of the world if you study them carefully. We are sympathetic to these situations, as many innocent people suffer, especially young children. Krishna of Hinduism said in the Bhagavad Gita, 'I come in every age to put the things right when sins go out of control.' God lets the system run on its own accord, as it has been designed to educate the soul, as long as the soul gets the education it needs and returns to its creator.

This is the will of God.

# BABA NAND SINGH JI

Baba Nand Singh was one of the greatest soul travellers of the last century. He was based in the district of Ludhiana, Punjab, India. He was born in Sherpur Kalan, which is not more than three miles from my birthplace. His preaching place was called Nanak Sar, less than 3 miles from where I lived during my childhood. Although he passed away ten years before my birth, I still consider him my first guru. His teachings significantly impacted people's minds and they are still in good circulation today.

When I came to know myself as a child, I listened to his stories from my elders at the age of six or seven years and I felt I should follow in his footsteps. Three days before my birth, he appeared to my grandmother and predicted my birth, telling her about my future. I must have been seven years old when my grandmother revealed this to me, which further impacted me. Some of my elders are still around to verify this statement.

I began to make plans to go about doing what he did, such as learning his hardcore meditation techniques, which were hard to follow. I could understand the physical side of the methods. Until today, the spiritual side remained secret because he never passed this information on to anybody; his followers were not ready to understand. Most of the followers were interested in material gains.

As I did not learn the spiritual techniques; my plans never materialised. He was a devotee of Guru Nanak and using trial-and-error methods; he managed to see the guru. Upon seeing his devotion, one day, Guru Nanak appeared to him and gave him a mission to follow, to spread Sikhism in the proper way, which he did, offering a new lead to Sikh followers. He revived all the old principles, which had been nearly forgotten or diluted to the point where they were no longer effective.

He was a great soul. I was impressed by Guru Nanak's appearance to him. Luckily, at the age of nine, I was fortunate enough to see Guru Nanak myself. He appeared where I was sleeping, woke me up and led me to a special place in our village; he appeared on a stage similar to a theatre.

He revealed his life from birth as a child, then as a teenager, youth, middle-aged and older man, until his last days in this world. Guru Nanak revealed his life in such detail that I can still go over and over it after all these years. I have described our meeting point with sketches in our book, The Will of God.

Baba Nand Singh Ji taught complete detachment. He was never married, never had his house and never touched money with his hands. He had just enough clothes to fulfil his needs. He never gathered food for the long term. He ate little, just enough to survive. He held a very high state of consciousness most of the time. He meditated eight to ten hours daily, apart from maintaining a higher consciousness.

All this was stirring in me the will to do something worthwhile. Leading an everyday life like anybody else seemed abnormal and I still feel the same. He was the first person to bring a spiritual spark into my life. The person who took over from him was Baba Isher Singh and he built a big temple at the same place where Baba Nand Singh used to stay and meditate. As I was growing up, I used to visit the temple often. I used to go there every evening and stay overnight, coming home in the morning to attend school.

I have done this for four years, from 7 October 1963 to 7 October 1967. From the age of ten to fourteen years. My thoughts were always on the words and examples set by this great saint. One evening, I was standing alone at one particular place and I heard a voice saying to me, 'If you want peace, there's plenty here but the thing you are looking for, you will not get it from here.' So, at the age of fourteen, I came to London to join my brother and father.

I was about twenty-two when I came across Sri Paul Ji's teachings from America. I read one of his books and immediately knew that my jigsaw puzzle was complete. All the missing pieces from my puzzle were in his teachings. The name Tiger's Fang implies that you must first pull the tiger's fang before you can claim to be the hunter.

This is a challenge to all future Seekers. So, I thank my first guru for leading me to my present one. Therefore, very sincerely, I dedicate these few lines to his memory.

# GOD-REALISATION

God-realisation is the Seeker's ultimate goal but only a few can achieve it in this lifetime. Self-realisation is the journey from the physical plane to the entry point of the soul plane. While experiencing lower planes and their activities to balance the five passions of the mind, the realisation comes that we are more than physical bodies. This is where we could say, 'I am soul,' knowing that psychic bodies are merely sheaths for the soul's survival in the lower planes.

We go through several situations to achieve experience in the lower worlds. This experience is registered in the soul's records and helps us attain maturity. With Self-realisation, your view of life changes and you learn that the physical is only your temporary house. Once we come to know ourselves as a soul, the next step of the journey is to understand, 'What the soul is? All religions claim that the soul is part of our creator, God. 'How can we know?

The only way to know this is to be bold and adventuresome. To achieve Self-realisation, we become soul travellers. We travel from the physical to the astral, causal and mental plane. The word 'travel' is inserted because we are subject to matter, energy, space and time in the lower worlds. We are not subject to matter, energy, space and time in the worlds of being. The soul will mock up the place to be and the being-ness of the soul takes place at the desired location.

This is a physical expression, as there are no desires in the higher planes. Being-ness is always on the move according to the duties allotted to the soul. A soul is a unit of God-awareness; the soul plane is the natural home for the soul. Satnam Ji is the Master of this universe. He is the first personification of God and his soul looks like a male embodiment and is responsible for all the souls ever created.

All souls, which come in different forms, such as insects, birds and animals, eventually end up in the soul plane and similarly, they all maintain their individuality. The soul can take shape in the lower worlds as it changes with time. When a child is born, it will appear as a child and as this child grows old in this world, it will appear as an older man. As some souls do appear to their relations for some reason, they appear as they looked physically before departing from this world.

The same soul is born as a child in a different world; it will appear with a new look. The soul will explore the soul plane as the soul itself. Under the guidance of your Master and the instruction of Satnam Ji. Once the soul has gained enough experience on the soul plane, the Master will prepare your journey to the next plane called Alakh-Lok. This time, you are under the instructions of Alakh-Purukh.

Alakh-Purukh and your Master will work in full cooperation because they have assumed the responsibility of bringing out the best in you. You have shown the potential to deliver your best; otherwise, the whole experience will not occur. While still living on the physical, you have to maintain your state of consciousness and your guru works hard to make sure you do that.

He will create obstacles, not to fail you but to refine your state of consciousness to a higher level; otherwise, the positive element is not possible. While on a higher plane, he ensures that the situation is perfect for achieving the experience. This is called the 'designer experience.' The soul always lives in the present moment. It does not matter on which plane it dwells, even from physical to the God-worlds. Only your lower bodies are subject to past, present and future.

Soul exists on the higher planes, such as the soul plane or above; it comes to living in a state of being-ness for the first time. This is the true spiritual statement. As we say on the physical, 'Be yourself and let the others be.' This means achieving freedom for yourself and granting the same to others. Being ourselves helps to begin our journey from the physical to the soul plane.

The actual state of being-ness is from the soul plane to the God-worlds, achieving God-realisation. Upon good experience on the Alakh-Lok, your Master will prepare you for your next adventure in Alaya-Lok. This is the seventh plane in God's world. Those saints or souls who manage to venture this far are indeed fortunate. It is an outstanding achievement and they deserve to be called saints or prophets.

They feel and know that all the lower worlds are at their disposal. The lord of this higher plane is called Alaya-Purukh. You may have noticed that all the higher planes and the lords' names are the same. They have achieved so much spiritually that the planes are named after them or God honour them for their achievements. The saint I used to follow in my childhood often commented to say he was the 'achiever of seven planes' (using different terminology).

None of his followers understood this. Nor did I. However, since I opened up to spiritual studies, I learned about his spiritual adventures. Once I asked my Master about that saint. Although he had passed away in the early sixties, my Master remarked, 'Yes, that man did become Spirit.' He commented during one of our inner journeys. Becoming Spirit means he achieved God-realisation.

Back to the seventh plane, Alaya-Lok. On 13 July 1980, I asked my Master, 'I want to know the truth.' After a short time, he took me to Alaya-Lok and said, 'This is the plane of truth.' I had a depth experience on this particular plane. What I saw it was completely different from the lower worlds. It is tough to explain in full detail. All I can say, this is the plane of truth. With the permission of Alaya-Purukh, we entered the next plane.

The Hakikat-Lok is the following realisation. Hakikat-Purukh is in charge of that plane. My Master introduced me to the lord of this plane and he showed me around for a long time. After having this experience, I wanted to go to the next plane but my Master said, 'No, we are staying here for tonight.' We'll make a move in the morning; which means not yet. I agreed. It is a physical expression; there is no night or darkness on this plane. There is only everlasting brilliance.

This is what you experience on your eighth journey and you are one step away from God-realisation. This was back in the 1980s and I was progressing quickly. I don't know whether it was my hard work or the Spirit wanted me to go at this speed. I remember the lord making the preparations for our stay that day. It was 3 January 1981. With the help of my Master, I made my way into Agam-Lok, the plane where one has a total experience of soul awareness.

This is the peak time for the individual. You are the picture of purity. You are like a mirror, reflecting the Spirit of God all the time and you will feel and say, 'Yes, I have achieved it.' Now you are a unit of God-awareness. You have achieved God-realisation. You have achieved nothing; you only became aware of what you already had. All we have to do is unfold ourselves to become aware of it.

We apply the word 'there' in the lower worlds, which is never 'here' because 'there' means 'somewhere else.' In the higher world, we use the term 'here.' Wherever we want to be, we will be here. This is the state of being-ness we use or apply in the higher worlds. It is a state of 'is-ness.' Even in the lower worlds, when we say the soul lives in the present time, we mean that it lives in the is-ness state of consciousness. It is the same continuity of is-ness but it becomes the past if we measure time by employing the clock.

The 'future' does not exist when we live in the present moment. It is always is-ness, here and now, which is the state of being-ness. Going from one plane to the next does not take any time. It is a state of being-ness from point A to point B. Agam-Lok is the ninth plane. The people who managed to come this far are the achievers of God-realisation and they have entered into the line of the ancient order of the Vairaagy Masters. Without the guidance of the Master, nothing is possible.

This is the furthest a person can go if subject to the physical body. A few chosen ones assigned special duties can progress to the next plane, known as Anami-Lok and further up, to the higher God's world. Nothing is impossible. All you have to do is work hard and with luck, you will find the spiritual

Master who can go this far himself. You can go this far but you must detach yourself from everything.

In my terminology, you have to walk even over yourself!

This is God-Realisation.

# WHO AM I?

This is the question I have asked myself so many times. I know I am a soul and a physical being at this present moment. I am talking about the success of my soul and physical being that I have achieved spiritually. Every person has a dream to materialise in this life but only a few will manage it; the rest will pass their time and be gone. There is always an opportunity in this life or the next. We can grasp it or wait at the seashore while nothing happens.

I've had the same dream since I was a child. 'Did I create this myself or was it attached to me by the Spirit to follow on? The latter seems to be the answer. I know many who are struggling. 'Why am I successful? I was lucky to set my foot on the spiritual side and I came to know my Master at a reasonably early age. Progress was so fast and so were my efforts. I put everything on the side and my main aim was to follow my dream. Every experience came faster than I expected.

I think the Master was more interested in me than I could imagine. It seemed as though the Master was on a mission himself. He showed me the maximum he could have and I was always prepared and waiting for him every moment of the day and night. Even during my working hours, I never lost sight of him. Now I believe he has found the perfect student, as I have in him the best Master. We were a good team and still, we are together.

I cannot prove who I am but some people do see glimpses of me on the spiritual side and report back. I achieved my success, which is only for me to know and others to find out. The question arises within, which I have asked myself several times, 'Do you know who you are? I know who I am but I ponder upon it. Many have asked this question over the centuries upon achieving their goal but disbelieving they have done it.

It is similar to any Olympian competing against other world athletes to win a gold medal. Upon victory, he exhibits all emotions because he does not believe he has accomplished his lifelong mission. We do not compete against anybody to achieve our spiritual goal but the whole world is competing against you, trying to stop you and deny us success. The negative force will use all the tools available in the box, such as the five passions of the mind and other negative entities but the strongest of all will be your family.

This is a lot harder than winning a gold medal. Like any athlete, you have to stay in top shape. The achievement is not of this world but the universes beyond. This is the path of knowingness and for the knowers. When the Master's mission is complete, you know all, as the Master does. Then you are the torch carrier, just like in the Olympics, until you reach your destination and the next one is ready to take over.

Book knowledge is good for intellectuals, as it does activate your imagination to seek further. It is your good karma that will eventually lead you to your destiny. The Master will appear when the soul is ready. This meeting is the starting point to knowing the truth, as the question is often asked; 'What is the truth? or 'What is reality? The answer has always been 'You must find out for yourself.' It cannot be explained or written down.

It has been written down in spiritual scriptures but in a diluted form of expression. As so many believe, it is not beyond reach; it is here or there for everyone to experience. No one can deny this truth from you. It is yours to have and experience and upon your success, it might surprise you and you will say, 'Have I done it?

'Do you know what you are and who you are?

The answer is within. 'Yes, I know. I Am.'

# ANAMI-LOK

Anami Lok means the 'nameless plane' or 'plane beyond description.' This is not the last plane of God but one of the highest in the second grand division of God and beyond reach in one lifetime. This is the tenth plane from the physical. All these planes individually contain hundred and thousands of planes within. The tenth plane is not to be confused with the tenth door. The God of itself is much higher than this and it is not within the grasp of its creation, although, at the same time, it is everywhere.

In my search, spanning over forty years, I knew a few beings who explored up to the fourteenth plane. This level of achievement is only for those Masters who God directly sends. There is always one Master responsible for all the planes, from the physical and up to the sixteenth plane. His minimum approach is up to the twelfth plane unless we are talking about some other Masters, who are numerous in this world.

Very few people will know this Master. Once this person is chosen for the Master-ship, he is taken to Anami Lok. Other Masters are also present at Anami Lok; they too are directly responsible to God or known as such. They are responsible for giving the final cleanliness to the soul body of this new Master-to-be. You will not see each other as souls or even as sparks on this plane but you are aware of each other's presence.

The soul is always pure but this ritual (physical expression) is only for the chosen one. The nine super souls came on 9 October 1981 to take me away to this plane. It is the final cleanliness of the soul body, not the physical body, which is left behind on this plane. You lie down, in a sense. These Masters are mighty and they begin to dismantle your soul body into millions and billions of atoms. The Masters are at task. You can feel their spiritual hands moving about.

It is a very strange feeling. It is a unique sensation you have never felt before; it is a very warm and pleasant feeling. There is no pain or pleasure during this process but happiness, of course. The soul is a unit of God-awareness. You are fully aware of what is taking place and you can sense all the atoms (brilliant micro-sized stars) of your soul body floating about. Once these Masters are satisfied, they re-assemble your soul body as before and you feel whole again and are on your feet, as they say.

Finally, they bring you back to where your physical body is lying on the bed. Then these Masters move on to their following tasks, which are many. This is an exceptional plane for souls. As mentioned before, Anami-Purukh, the ruler of this plane, is responsible for creating new souls, as Satnam Ji is the caretaker of souls. I have not read the Guru Granth of Sikhism but I know Anami Lok is written in this holy book by Sri Guru Nanak.

All is in your grasp if you take an adventure in the world of being.

# SPIRITUAL MASTER AND I

My first guru led me to an imagination of the subjective worlds. My new Master turned that imagination into reality and the journey began. My seeking for the Master finished. My search and unique Master's teaching fit like a hand in a glove but even better. As soon as I posted the letter to become a member, I had a strange feeling, as if someone were walking along with me.

I could not see it but I could feel the Spirit's presence. I had my proof when he said, 'I am always with you and as close as your heartbeat.' During meditation, he used to make his appearance one way or the other with a slight touch on the shoulder or a blissful feeling on the spiritual eye. He would show me spiritual light or make me hear the sound. First, he introduced me to Fubi-kants, the guardian of the spiritual city known as Katsu-pari Monastery, a way-station to the subjective worlds.

Next, he introduced me to Yabal Sakabi, who wore a sunset colour robe. He is about my height and has no hair on his head. He is the guardian of Agam-Des; this is another way-station to the subjective world. I met Banjani Ji and his spiritual place is in the Gobi Desert, Mongolia. He is slightly dark in colour, with a striking gaze and a pleasant smile.

We proceeded to the astral plane and visited the temple of Golden Wisdom, where we met the guardian of the temple and the lord of that plane. Then we went to the causal plane and underwent the same routine, meeting the lords and listening to the sound of that plane. The mental and subconscious planes followed and we proceeded to the soul plane. We have been to these planes several times so I could get familiarised.

He never let me down whenever I asked for favours to help my friends or family members. Sometimes I pushed myself over the limit in my asking. Still, he did not let me down. But in those circumstances, I promised him to take on their karmas myself, which takes its toll on the physical body. Maybe later, I can provide examples. One time, I asked him, 'What is deep samadhi?

He took me into meditation and raised my vibrations to the level of bliss state so I could have the experience. It was the same with telepathy, a natural gift to me since my early days. I could communicate with the people who were very close to my heart. My inner communication with Spirit was so strong that 'instant' would be the right word for it.

As soon as I focused on communicating on any subject with the spiritual Master, I received the answer instantly. The Master is always here to communicate. It is always up to us to raise the vibration level at the inner. From 1979 to 1981 was my golden period with the spiritual Master, as we travelled a lot to the inner worlds. I received the ninth initiation on 3 January 1981.

The spiritual goal we set earlier did not materialise in October 1981. I was a little disappointed and sent a letter. There was no reply on the physical plane but he appeared, as usual, on the spiritual level but as far as I am concerned, an evasive answer was given. Answer; This time was, just in case we need you but Paul and I are training you for 1986.

I knew this was not true but I took the answer gracefully and went into silence. After that, the whole structure of the organisation changed and with that, future goals also vanished into thin air. Most of our internal or spiritual conversations are recorded in my diary, The Will of God. I kept my silence all these years. I did not wish to discuss this with anyone. This was my private world.

I have been trained to maintain this kind of stamina by the ancient Masters. Paul had described my character and age in a few places. Nowadays, considering my age, I have been refusing since early 2001. I believe the chance should be given to someone young so the new person can carry on for longer. The Spirit did not accept my request. All I can say now is, 'So be it.'

It is the same in the future; the Spirit will take its course and choose the person from whatever colour or nation it suits. We cannot dictate to the Spirit what to do, as this is impossible. Even if we try, we have to pay the consequences. Some people claim to be present Masters. I wish them all the best, as I have no right to enter into someone's psychic space and tell them what to do.

That will be a violation of spiritual law. Because of what happened last time, my Master did not want to make the decision physically and let the Spirit take its course. I also have been taking my time to let people decide first what they want in life. Maybe that is the way Spirit works. After the soul plane, he took me to Alakh, Alaya, Hakikat-Lok. I was introduced to all the lords of these planes.

I listened to spiritual discourses given by these lords as they poured the words of wisdom into my soul. After long discourses, I was delighted and asked my guru, 'Are we going to the next plane? He said, 'No, your experience is not yet finished here.' Next, we were in Agam-Lok. I heard the sound of woodwinds and listened to a spiritual discourse by the lord of this plane. My next journey was to Anami Lok, where I was introduced to Anami-Purukh.

The experience of this plane is written in the chapter 'Anami-Lok.' The experiences with the Master are numerous and most of the journeys are beyond description. They are published in our book, 'The Will of God.' We had enjoyable times together. He gave healing to my body, as I had damaged a few parts here and there. He used to appear at my bedside, wake me up and apply healings to the affected body parts. Warm and pleasant waves surged into that part of the body and it healed instantly.

In the next chapter, I will give you an example of how to communicate with the Master, how he answers back, how he heals and how he can back up his disciple. This fantastic story details a continuous experience for over three months. This story was published in 1979 (in E. Mata Journal, volume 4) under the headline, 'A Call for Help,' on page 35. I still hold a copy but I was not happy with its illustration.

It was all twisted; I felt this magnificient experience was not justified. I rewrote the entire experience again and sent it to the office. Now I will share it with you. I have obtained written consent to publish from the person involved. This experience and hundreds of others regarding healing, telepathy, divine light and sound and other journeys are written in my private diary.

# EXPERIENCE

This experience will show the result of successful communication and having total reliance upon the spiritual Master and what he can do for the followers. I never felt the urge to see him physically as he was always around spiritually.

## Borrowed Vision

My friend, Mr Singh, had a car accident on the M1 motorway. Both of his eyes were severely damaged, especially the left eye. The windscreen smashed into small pieces and glass went inside his both eyes. The left eye was ultimately damaged. I went to see him at Watford Hospital because we were very close friends and had close family relations. He knew that I was following a spiritual Master, so he asked me if I could request him to get help.

I requested the Master for help during my evening meditation. I also used to take small naps (learned earlier) to get instant guidance from the Master. I received the consent and I promised that my Master would help him. The senior surgeon operated on both of his eyes. The doctor called me and his younger brother Mr M. Singh to his flat, offered us a cup of tea and told us the total damage. He said that he had removed everything from his left eye. The doctors' flat was within the Hospital compound.

Mr Singhs' right eye is also severely damaged but later on, he would not have a hundred percent vision but he would have seventy percent vision, which is now confirmed. So, Mr Singh could not see anything from his left eye when the bandages were removed. But he could see a shadow vision through his right eye. But the doctors had told us that he would soon develop a cataract in his right eye.

The doctor said; that it would take at least three months to develop a cataract before he could remove it entirely. He did not want to discuss the left eye because he had already told us the condition. After a few days, the vision from his right eye began to disappear as the cataract began to develop. Mr Singh got scared as his world was turned into darkness. He was disappointed and depressed and began to cry over my shoulder.

He asked; If my Master could help him see through his left eye while the cataract was developing in the right eye. Mr Singh was not aware of his left eye condition because we never told him or the doctor. We did not want to break his heart. But anyway; I got a bit emotional and said I would ask him if he could give him the 'Sight' for that period until his right eye began to see again.

## Spiritual Master Agreed

So, as the shadowed vision disappeared from the right eye, the vision began to appear in his left eye. Later the vision from his right eye disappeared entirely but there was enough vision in the left eye. After discharge, we had a follow-up appointment with the leading surgeon who initially operated. I went with Mr Singh as an interpreter as usual. When our turn came, the doctor called us in. He checked his right eye and remarked; Blah-Blah, his cataract is developing okay.

Then I broke the news and said, doctor, 'Do you know, this man can see through his left eye? 'Can you imagine the doctors' face? It got red and he said to me, showing both of his hands, palms up, I have removed everything from his left eye with these two hands. 'How can he possibly see from his left eye? I said; okay. But I put the challenge on the doctor to test his left eye. He agreed and tested his vision and Mr Singh reads the big letters in no time. 'The doctor never raised the question to know how?

The doctor was so pleased; he gave him the thickest glasses so that he could see and Mr Singh began to see even better. He walked the streets of Southall, Middx, without any assistance or stick for a good three months. His cataract developed fully and the same surgeon removed the cataract and after a few days, his vision began to re-appear in his right eye properly and began to disappear from his left eye. He never saw again from his left eye.

That was a gift from the Spirit. During that period, I received spiritual guidance daily and moment to moment. The guidance was shared with Mr Singh and his family regarding when, date, time and what would happen. Every day's guidance came true a hundred percent and even more. Now you can count the number of days and the number of experiences I or we had.

'Can you imagine what we learned during this period? 'Can you imagine what Spirit is all about and what it can do? Everything was done with a hundred percent faith in the Spirit. We can move mountains with faith; It was total reliance upon Spirit. It Just Is. I have learned over the years that when people have problems, they get emotional and cry on your shoulder. In return, you give it your best to ensure they get help.

They forget who you are and who the Master was when they are healed. I am not a person who is looking for too many thank-yous. As a courtesy, I appreciate Spirit. As the requester and the middleman, I took the load of karma on myself; otherwise, it is not as easy to materialise this kind of experience. The requesters never reveal much to anybody, as they are working for the good of the whole.

With experience, I have learned (maybe the hard way) that it is better to leave these people alone and let them reap what they sow. Leave their destiny in the hands of the Spirit. As the requester has diverted justice, suffering is bound to happen within their physical body. On the other hand, we are lovers of all life. We just cannot stop helping. I could write a book on 'Spiritual Master and I. Spirit; It just is.

# THE SEEKER IS A FAILURE

Our failures are many because we want God according to our set conditions. We were spiritually hungry and that hunger led us from one teacher to another. Eventually, we found one. We follow the teachings sincerely and every day is a miracle. It was your sincerity and effort which was responsible for miracles to happen. In the beginning, all Seekers have several dreams to fulfil, such as spiritual freedom, soul travel, seeing other worlds and eventually becoming assistants with God for its cause.

I have seen people spend more than thirty years with a good teacher and fantastic teachings but nothing solid materialises for them. As a gesture of love, some experiences are given by the Master to maintain their faith. The Master is available if the Seeker puts in the effort. However, a minor effort is not good enough compared to the goals you have set for yourself. If you want to become a saint, you have to materialise these qualities within yourself to hold this type of consciousness.

With your efforts and the Master's guidance, inner communication is established so you can communicate with each other. If you cannot communicate whenever you like with the spiritual Master, you have not made much progress. Your journey is almost at a standstill. This communication must be established with the present Master, not one who has departed from this world. If you disagree with this statement, I don't think you understand the teachings you are following.

However, at present, your effort is not even reasonable enough to clear your daily karma. It is a challenging task to become a saint. Most likely don't realise that you are working on three lives simultaneously. First, you are working off your previous lives' karma. Second, you are working off or balancing out karma which is being created daily. Third, you have to put extra effort into materialising your goal, which you have set for yourself.

If your effort in the first or second stage is similar to any sports results; the match is a draw. If you want to win, you have to score extra goals. We are not in competition with anyone. It is the competition within. Keep striving towards your goal to achieve self or God-realisation. It is a continuous effort, every day, for life. You cannot afford to miss your mark every single day. The failure points for the Seekers are many. We want to have God the way we want it. No one can dictate the Spirit and have success.

To succeed, you have to work with the Spirit so closely that you breathe, eat and sleep Spirit. Let the Spirit be the driving force behind all the actions of life. All the situations and karma will work off in no time. The Master can give Self-realisation instantly if the Seeker is ready. Otherwise, with good effort, five years is too long. I have seen people go to church and temple on Sunday, wearing their respective religious costumes. If you watch them closely, it seems as if all the saints have landed on this planet Earth.

In the late afternoon, they all change their costumes. Now it is party time. At times, we want to be Romeo and Juliet. Millionaires, politicians, you name it, we want to do it all. The temptations of this world are many. Over-indulgence in any action will take you off the track. People hardly try to work out the five passions of the mind. We want to gain everything spiritually but do not want to lose anything materially. You cannot have it both ways. Few people are doing or participating in all the negative acts.

Possibly, they can and they think they can get away with it. The answer is no and the Kal force has grounded you with minimum effort. Intellectuals are trying to imagine reality with the mind. You have to rise above the mental. Truth cannot be analysed; it is to be experienced. It is a continuous effort to work towards your weak points. You can hide everything from others but you cannot hide anything from God or yourself. God and within yourself are identical to each other.

Within is part of it, known as the spiritual spark. Any person can bounce back at any time. Do not give up. A positive attitude, regular spiritual exercises and continuous inner communication with the Spirit will bring success. If your efforts are poor, it does not matter what teachings or Master you follow; nothing will materialise. The Master is there to guide you but it cannot walk for you. If you are sincere, nothing can stand between you and God. You are face to face with its reality.

The choice is yours.

# THE POWER OF ASSUMPTION

The key to having a successful spiritual life is the law of assumption and how you apply it in your life. This is the last chapter and I believe it was the missing piece of the puzzle. The answers are always evasive no matter whom you approach for spiritual secrets. Maybe they do not know the answers themselves. You are the Knower of the truth and continue your efforts and at the same time, apply the law of assumption; success will be yours.

A positive attitude is vital for your assumption to materialise. In the beginning, you imagine or make-believe the Master will appear in the third-eye. In the background is your assumption, which acts as a transformer to accomplish your goal. If you believe in your attempt, the Master will appear. The same can be applied to seeing the light or hearing the sound. The law of assumption can be applied to achieve Self or God-realisation. You assume I am now a Self or God-realised person.

At the same time, you are doing your homework to create the qualities and responsibilities that go with this state of consciousness. No one can dictate to the Spirit; what to do or when to do it. Your sincerity, patience and hard work will bring the fruits of your efforts. Do not be surprised; you will find yourself dwelling in this state of consciousness one day. You have achieved nothing new. With your effort, you have become aware of what you already had.

Those searching for God go from teacher to teacher; if lucky, the realisation may come. It is within us all the time. Once you realise God's presence within, you can enjoy a state of bliss. Life is based on the theory of karma. Bad karmas are often irritating and give you rough times. During a rough patch of life, you can apply the power of assumption to bring some positivity to your life. Apply this principle and your problems will be much less than they used to be or would have been.

You have prepared yourself to face the disaster with a positive attitude. The problem may still exist but mentally, you have become stronger than the problem itself. This is why we use the phrase; 'A change in the state of consciousness is required.' 'Do you know that when the state of consciousness changes, the karma theory working upfront is now working in the background? If the assumption of anything dominates your feeling most of the waking hours, the attainment of your goal is inevitable.

Mentally, you have already achieved it; now, you are just waiting for it to materialise. A negative attitude or feeling is the killer of any achievement in life. In the beginning, your thoughts were crowded with many positive and negative ideas. Once you eliminate all of them, your main idea comes to dominate and soon, your goal will materialise. Your faith can move mountains. Some people have very strong willpower. 'What is willpower? It is a strong belief within yourself.

You believe in yourself and assume everything will be fine. Over the centuries, people have conquered even deadly ailments such as cancer thanks to willpower. The flow of Spirit within your body is responsible for vitality, apart from your food, vitamins and minerals. If there is no Spirit in your body, it is declared dead. The flow of positive spiritual atoms will change the chemistry of the physical body. Once vibrations are raised to the level of the soul plane, then surge to any body part for a few minutes or heal someone else.

Physical touch is not recommended. The focus is applied in a similar way to a laser beam. Before quitting, assume it is healed and mentally or physically say, 'Well, it is done. I leave this in the hands of the Spirit.' You can apply this power of assumption during any negative or psychic attacks. Say it in your own words; 'Nothing can touch me.' You can also create a positive aura around you, like a circle, by chanting your spiritual word, creating dots until they form a ring.

No psychic entity will dare to enter your psychic ring unless you break the loop with the fear factor. Most world-class leaders were born ordinary, just like anybody else. At a certain age, they believed that they could do better. They assumed the role of that character in which they grew with time and people came to know who they were. The power of assumption, which they applied knowingly or unknowingly, brought them success. Most people carry a negative attitude and say, 'I cannot do this or that.'

People with a negative attitude will not go very far in life. If you do not want to leave your shell, there is nothing anyone can do for you. The role of assumption in your life is to direct all your actions, consciously or unconsciously, in one direction, very similar to a magnet. It is a setback for the follower to use the power of assumption to gain a bank balance, a better partner or a job. You can achieve many things via assumptions where the application of force does not work.

To materialise your goal, the persistence of wish fulfilment should be in a balanced manner. When that happens, your goal materialises. I have worked very hard to fulfil my goal. I believed in myself and everything became possible in this lifetime. I applied the law of assumption with every action. Since I was a child, I knew I could achieve success in spirituality and assumed such a role within myself. In my own right, I am successful. In this book, what I have written is only a tiny percentage of what I can write. There is a lot more to come; Good readings to you.

God Bless All

SHER GILL Galib

London

Lightning Source UK Ltd.
Milton Keynes UK
UKHW040738020123
414708UK00001B/18